# EVERYDAY READING
# INFORMATION TOOLS

**EVERYDAY READING SERIES**

AGS
PUBLISHING

Circle Pines, Minnesota 55014-1796
800-328-2560
www.agsnet.com

**Publisher's Project Staff**

Vice President, Product Development: Kathleen T. Williams, Ph.D., NCSP; Associate Director, Product Development: Teri Mathews; Editor: Judy Monroe; Assistant Editor: Sarah Brandel; Development Assistant: Bev Johnson; Creative Services Manager: Nancy Condon; Senior Designer: Daren Hastings; Project Coordinator/Designer: Laura Henrichsen; Desktop Production Artist: Peggy Vlahos; Materials Management: Carol Nelson; Marketing Director: Brian Holl

Development and writing services by Ellen McPeek Glisan

© 2004 AGS Publishing
4201 Woodland Road, Circle Pines, MN 55014-1796
800-328-2560 • www.agsnet.com

AGS Publishing is a trademark and trade name of American Guidance Service, Inc.

All rights reserved, including translation. No part of this publication may be reproduced or transmitted in any form or by any means without written permission from the publisher.

Printed in the United States of America

Product Number 92130
ISBN 0-7854-3671-5

A 0 9 8 7 6 5 4 3 2

# CONTENTS

Introduction .........................4

## Unit 1: Bus Schedules
Lesson 1— Taking the Airport Bus ........8
Lesson 2— Your Own Bus Schedule ......13

## Unit 2: Telephone Books
Lesson 3— Page from the
 Telephone Book ............18
Lesson 4— Your Own Telephone
 Book Page ................23

## Unit 3: Recipes
Lesson 5— Avocado Dip, Fruit Dump
 Cake, and Beef Tacos ........28
Lesson 6— Your Own Recipe ...........33

## Unit 4: Dictionaries
Lesson 7— Dictionary Page .............38
Lesson 8— Your Own Dictionary Page ....43

## Unit 5: Indexes
Lesson 9— Work Sharp Office
 Products Index ..............48
Lesson 10— Your Own Index ...........53

## Unit 6: Tables of Contents
Lesson 11— *Make Your Own Crafts* Table
 of Contents ................58
Lesson 12— Your Own Table
 of Contents ................63

## Unit 7: Movie Schedules
Lesson 13— North Ring Theaters .........68
Lesson 14— Your Own Movie Schedules ...73

## Unit 8: Packing Slips
Lesson 15— Owls Computer
 Company...................78
Lesson 16— Your Own Packing Slip .......83

## Unit 9: Bank Statements
Lesson 17— Checking Account
 Statement .................88
Lesson 18— Your Own Bank
 Statement .................93

## Unit 10: TV Schedules
Lesson 19— Tuesday Evening ............98
Lesson 20— Your Own TV Schedule ......103

## Unit 11: Road Maps
Lesson 21— Maps of Connecticut ........108
Lesson 22— Your Own Road Map .......113

## Unit 12: Product Instructions
Lesson 23— Electronic Calculator ........118
Lesson 24— Your Own Product
 Instructions ...............123

## Summary of Skills and Strategies ...128

# Introduction

Reading is a part of every day in the world around you. Reading is like anything else that matters. To be good at it, you have to practice. *Everyday Reading: Information Tools* will help you be a better reader. You will also learn how to read important information so you can make wise choices.

What are **information tools**? Information tools are items such as books, charts, lists, and reports. When you want to know a fact, you can look at an information tool to find the answer. You might use an information tool to find a telephone number or a recipe. You are using an information tool when you read a map or movie schedule or watch television.

Using information tools makes it easier to do the things you want to do. So, it helps to read and understand these tools.

Here are the information tools you'll learn about in this book:

■ **Bus Schedules**
Every person who rides a bus has to know when and where the bus stops. Learn to read bus schedules so you can make plans.

■ **Telephone Books**
Do you need help spelling a name? Have you forgotten a telephone number? Do you need a friend's address? Telephone books put all this information at your fingertips.

■ **Recipes**
Do you like meatloaf, chicken soup, chocolate chip cookies, or banana bread? Can you think of something else that sounds good to eat? Recipes are great tools because they help you make all kinds of foods.

■ **Dictionaries**
Can you spell every word you use? Do you know the meaning of every word you read? Of course you don't. A dictionary is a great tool to find spellings and meanings of words.

■ **Indexes**
Many books and catalogs have indexes. Indexes make it easier to find information. Indexes are like the yellow pages in telephone books—information is grouped by topics in ABC order.

■ **Tables of Contents**

A table of contents is like an outline or map for a book. It shows the general ideas in order. You can learn a lot about a book by reading the table of contents.

■ **Movie Schedules**

Do you ever go to movies? Do you think your time is important? If so, knowing how to read movie schedules will be helpful to you.

■ **Packing Slips**

When you order something in the mail, you get a packing slip. It helps to know how to read a packing slip. You can learn a lot about your order and the company that sent your items from the packing slip.

■ **Bank Statements**

Banks can help keep your money safe and organized. Bank statements help you keep track of the money you put in a bank and the money you spend.

■ **TV Schedules**

Do you watch television? Reading TV schedules helps you find your favorite shows.

■ **Road Maps**

Road maps help people drive to and from most places without getting lost.

■ **Product Instructions**

How are a new TV, toaster, lawn mower, and hair dryer alike? They all come with instructions! Even when you think you know what to do, it is a good idea to read the instructions.

## PERSONAL READING GOALS

Set goals for yourself before you start this book. At the end of the book, come back to see how you did with your goals.

I want to learn more about _____

_____

_____

One thing in reading I want to be better at by the end of this book is

_____

_____

_____

## READING STRATEGIES

In this book, you will use reading strategies, reading comprehension skills, and critical thinking tools. You will learn to look at reading from different points of view. Here are some tips and strategies you can use to get started.

### Word Study: Five Steps to Learning a Word

1. **Read the word.** Notice its shape. Is it long or short? What letters does it begin with? Does it look like other words you know?

2. **Say the word.** What sounds does it have? Which letters stand for those sounds?

3. **Write the word.** Get a feel for the word by writing it down.

4. **Practice reading the word.** Read the word again and again until you know it.

5. **Use the word.** Add the word to your vocabulary, when you speak and when you write.

### Spelling Tips

Use these tips to help you spell correctly when you write:

- **Listen to the sounds.** Listen for the sounds you hear at the beginning, in the middle, and at the end of a word.

- **Think about letters.** Ask yourself: What letters or letter patterns usually stand for the sounds in this word?

- **Think about meaning.** Should you write **hair** or **hare**? Is the word you want spelled **won** or **one**? Thinking about how the word is used in a sentence helps you know which spelling to use.

- **Picture the word.** Make a mental picture of the word. Think about its shape and length.

- **Check the word.** Look at the word after you've written it. Does it look right? If you're not sure, look in a dictionary.

**Word Attack Tips**

Most short words are simple to read. When you come to longer words, it's easy to get stumped. Here are some tips that can help:

- **Look for word parts you know.** Is the word made up of a smaller word you know, plus an ending?

- **Look for letter patterns you know.** Knowing a pattern of letters can help you read other words with that pattern. If you can read **main,** then you are reading the **ain** letter pattern. This means you can also read **train, brain, stained,** and **raining**.

- **Break the word into parts.** Is the word made up of two smaller words that have been put together?

- **Look for syllables.** The vowels in a word are a clue to how many syllables (parts) it has.

- **Look at the letters in the word.** What sounds do the letters stand for? Blend all the sounds together to read the word.


**Reading Strategies**

A strategy is a smart plan for getting a job done. Reading strategies help with the job of reading. Here are some strategies you'll learn to use:

- **Preview and predict.** Looking ahead at your reading can help you know what to expect.

- **Set a purpose.** Every time you read, you do it for a reason. Knowing that reason can help you understand what you read.

- **Think critically.** Reading without thinking is like chewing without swallowing. What's the point? This worktext will show you how to think about what you read by asking yourself questions.

- **Use things you already know.** You probably know something about many things you read. Try to think about these things before you read. It makes reading more interesting.

- **Read actively.** When you are active, reading is more fun. This worktext will teach you to mark text, take notes, and ask questions.

# UNIT 1: BUS SCHEDULES

## Lesson 1 — BEFORE READING

## Taking the Airport Bus

### PHONICS

Some words end in blends. Final blends are two or three letters that together make a mixed sound. You hear sounds from each letter.

### VOCABULARY

**a.m.** (A.M.)
between midnight and noon

**connection**
a change to another bus, train, or plane

**depart**
to leave a station or stop

**p.m.** (P.M.)
between noon and midnight

### LIFE SKILLS

Many people take an airport bus to get to and from an airport. They need to know when and where the bus goes. They can find this information on a bus schedule.

### Letters and Sounds

**Read the blends in the box. Now add a blend to make the words below. The first two have been done for you.**

| ld | lp | lb | ft | ct | sk |
|----|----|----|----|----|----|
| lf | lt | ln | st | xt | sp |
| lk | lm | ls | nt | pt |    |

1. bu**lk**
2. bo**ld**
3. fa_____
4. ke_____
5. ga_____
6. sai_____
7. fi_____
8. ne_____
9. e_____
10. si_____
11. he_____
12. pe_____
13. hu_____
14. ri_____
15. swi_____
16. ki_____
17. wi_____

**Use the blends in the box below to make more words.**

| rt  | rk | rn | rp | nk |
|-----|----|----|----|----|
| rst | rb | rf | rs | nd |
| rd  | rm | rl | ng | mp |

1. ha_____
2. you_____
3. si_____
4. co_____
5. su_____
6. swi_____
7. tu_____
8. ca_____
9. fu_____
10. ri_____
11. cu_____
12. du_____
13. pa_____
14. bu_____
15. ra_____

### Use What You Know

**Answer the questions below.**

1. Have you ever taken an airport bus? Circle one.   Yes   No

2. If yes, would you take an airport bus again?   Yes   No

8   UNIT 1 • Lesson 1

# Lesson 1

**READING** Taking the Airport Bus

## Charlotte's Shuttle Bus Company

### CHARLOTTESVILLE ROUTE

| Departs | Dulles Airport | 2:05 P.M. | 5:35 P.M. | 7:05 P.M. |
|---|---|---|---|---|
| Arrives | Warrenton | 2:55 P.M. | 7:55 P.M. | |
| | Culpeper | 3:20 P.M. | 6:50 P.M. | 8:20 P.M. |
| | Charlottesville | 4:30 P.M. | 8:00 P.M. | 9:30 P.M. |
| | Lynchburg | 6:15 P.M. | | 11:15 P.M.* |
| | Roanoke | 7:30 P.M. | | 12:25 A.M.* |
| Departs | Roanoke | | 5:30 A.M. | |
| | Lynchburg | | 6:45 A.M. | 10:55 A.M.* |
| | Charlottesville | 6:20 A.M. | 8:30 A.M. | 12:45 P.M. |
| | Culpeper | 7:30 A.M. | 9:40 A.M. | 1:55 P.M. |
| | Warrenton | 7:50 A.M. | 10:00 A.M. | 2:15 P.M. |
| Arrives | Dulles Airport | 8:40 A.M. | 10:50 A.M. | 3:05 P.M. |

***Connection** at Charlottesville

# Lesson 1

## AFTER READING

## Taking the Airport Bus

**STRATEGY**

**Make It Clear** is a reading strategy. Use it to help you understand what you read. Understanding how information is put together helps you know what it says.

**READING COMPREHENSION**

Sometimes you can find a main idea and details for one part of a reading piece. The main idea of the part is often a detail for the overall main idea.

### Reading Comprehension

**Read the airport bus schedule on page 9. Then answer the questions below.**

1. **Study Text Features:** Why do you think asterisks (*) are on the bus schedule?

   _____

2. **Make It Clear:** Why do you think dark lines are on the bus schedule?

   _____

3. **Main Idea and Details:** In the chart below, write the cities the bus passes through on the way to the airport.

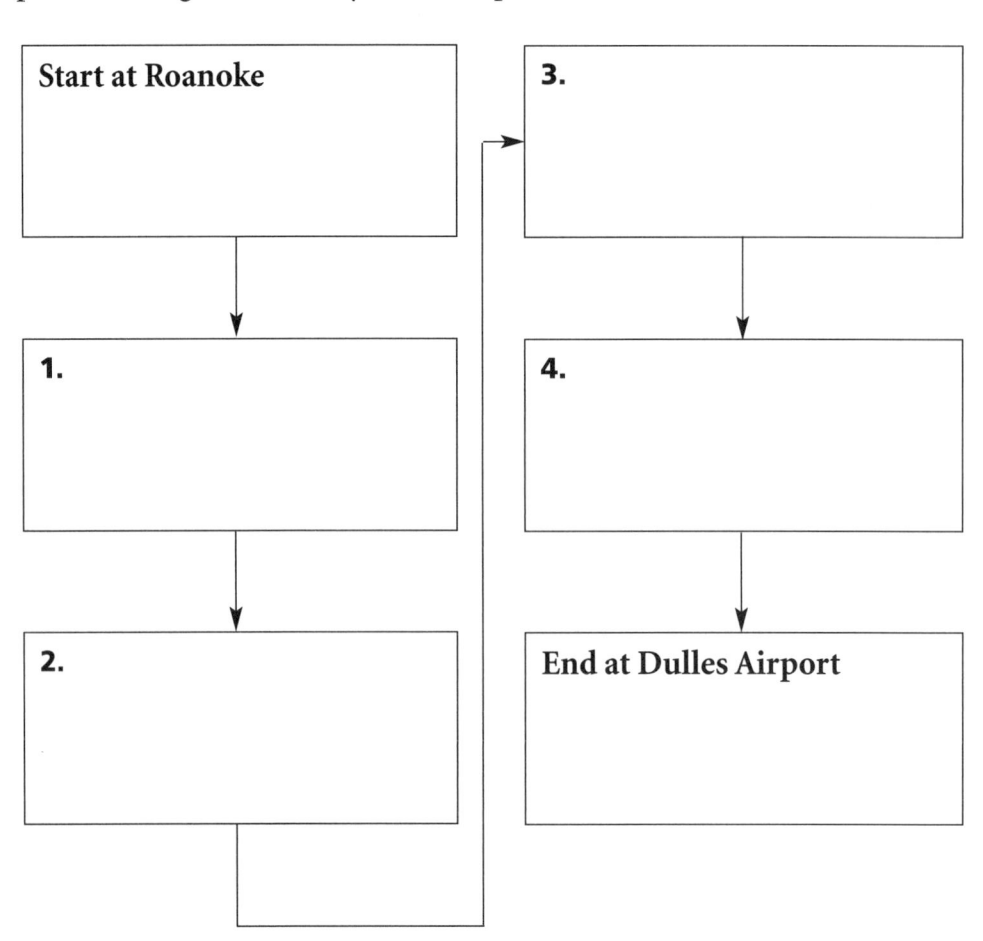

   | Start at Roanoke | 3. |
   |---|---|
   | 1. | 4. |
   | 2. | End at Dulles Airport |

4. **Make Connections:** Find the cities in Item 3 above on a map.

10 UNIT 1 • Lesson 1

## READING COMPREHENSION

In *Everyday Reading*, reading comprehension uses three types of activities:

- **Reading Strategies.** Ways to better understand information while reading
- **Reading Comprehension Skills.** Activities that use information from a reading piece
- **Critical Thinking Tools.** Steps to use in both reading and thinking

## Letters and Sounds Review

**Read the clues below. Think of words that end with a blend. Write the words in the puzzle.**

**Across**
1. A dog's wild cousin
3. Holds paper, pens, and a computer
5. Written words
7. To take a quick breath
9. A dog's hard breathing
11. Home to a camper

**Down**
2. To bend a paper
4. Now I keep, before I _____
6. The feeling of needing water
8. Used to make paper
10. To tip sideways

## LANGUAGE

Commas are needed in these places in sentences:

- Between the parts of a series or list
  **Example:** The girl had a dog, cat, and bird.
- Between a city and a state
  **Example:** I live in Salt Lake City, Utah.

## Language

**Add commas to the sentences below.**

1. Buses are a good way to get around if you are not late loud or rushed.

2. One big city with good buses is San Francisco California.

3. A small town like Winslow Illinois does not have buses.

4. If the bus fare is 75¢, you could pay with quarters dimes or nickels.

5. Local buses often go to shopping malls big companies and other large buildings.

6. Some buses go to airports big cities and tourist sites.

UNIT 1 • Lesson 1    11

## LIFE SKILLS

To brainstorm, gather together a bunch of ideas. Write down your ideas. Then work with your ideas to do what you want.

For example, you can organize your ideas to make sense of some information. Choose a way to organize that makes sense to you.

**Life Skills Focus**

**Brainstorm and Organize:** Think of seven tasks you need to do over the next seven days. Write the tasks on the lines below. Would taking a bus help you with the task? If yes, circle the task.

### My Seven Tasks

1. _____

2. _____

3. _____

4. _____

5. _____

6. _____

7. _____

# Lesson 2 BEFORE READING: Your Own Bus Schedule

## WORD SKILLS

A **suffix** is a word part added to the end of a word. Follow the patterns below to add the suffix *ed* or *ing*.

hop + p + ed = hopped
**and**
hop + p + ing = hopping

❖ ❖ ❖

rake − e + ed = raked
**and**
rake − e + ing = raking

❖ ❖ ❖

last + ed = lasted
**and**
last + ing = lasting

❖ ❖ ❖

hurry − y + i + ed = hurried
**but**
hurry − y + ing = hurrying

### Word Skills

**Read the Word Skills box to the left. Then read the words before each sentence. Add the suffix ed or ing to each word. Write the new word where it belongs.**

1. (ride)   Keep an eye on your things when _____ a bus.

2. (catch)   Leave by 4:00 if you are _____ the 4:30 bus.

3. (hand)   It's nice to say hello when you are _____ your money to the driver.

4. (stop)   Don't get off a bus until it has _____.

5. (work)   _____ people often take a bus twice a day.

6. (hurry)   He _____ and got to the bus station in time.

7. (ride, walk)   If you live far from where you are going, _____ the bus is better than _____.

### Use What You Know

**Tape, staple, or glue a bus schedule to page 14. Then answer the questions below.**

1. Have you used this bus schedule?   Yes   No

   If yes, where did you go? _____

   _____

2. Is this a local or airport bus schedule? _____

   How do you know? _____

   _____

UNIT 1 • Lesson 2    13

## Lesson 2 READING  Your Own Bus Schedule

**Find a bus schedule or make a copy of a bus schedule. Tape, staple, or glue the bus schedule to this page.**

# Lesson 2

## AFTER READING: Your Own Bus Schedule

**READING COMPREHENSION**

The **main idea** is the most important idea in a paragraph, passage, or page.

The main idea is often supported by **details**. Add up the details to help you figure out the main idea.

**CRITICAL THINKING**

Brainstorm to:
- remember things you know or saw
- think of things you're not sure of
- collect ideas

**CRITICAL THINKING**

To organize facts, choose the parts of the information that are meaningful to you. Then organize the parts in a way that helps you.

### Reading Comprehension

**Read your own bus schedule on page 14. Then answer the questions below.**

1. **Main Idea and Details:** Choose a stop on your bus schedule. What are four stops that come after this stop? Write the first stop and the four other stops below.

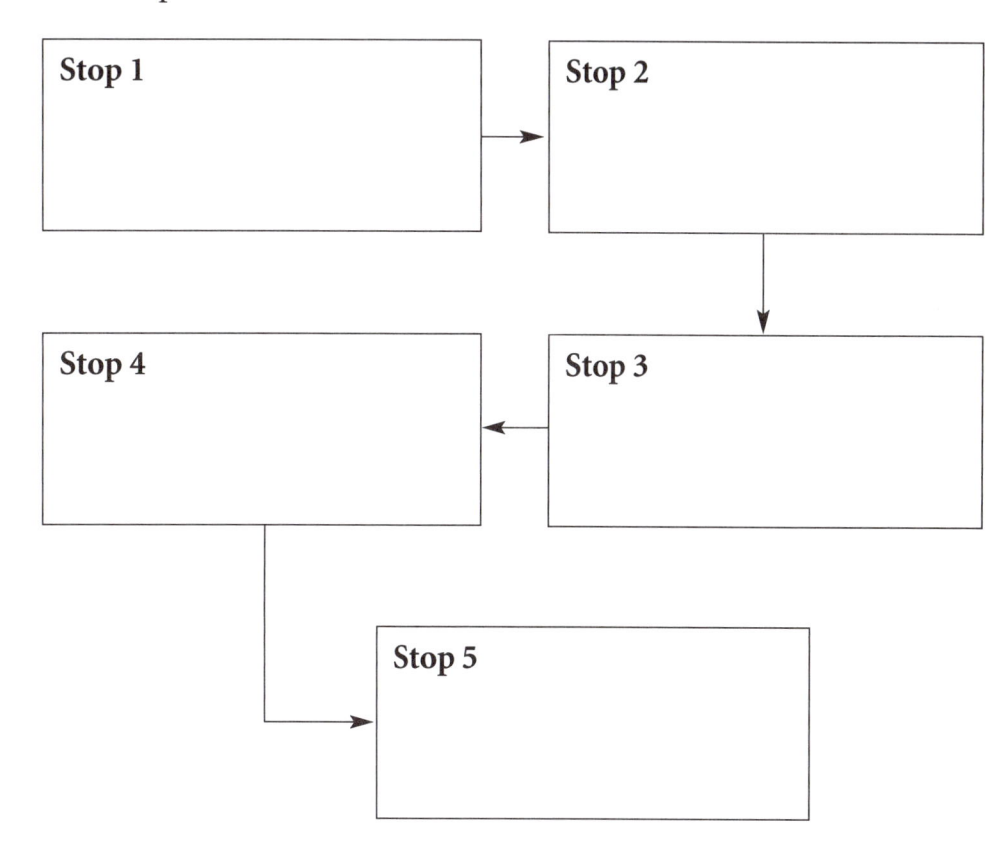

   Stop 1 → Stop 2 → Stop 3 → Stop 4 → Stop 5

2. **Brainstorm:** What are four different types of buses you have seen? Write them on the lines below.

   _____  _____

   _____  _____

3. **Organize Ideas:** On your own paper, write the name of a stop on your bus schedule. Create a new bus schedule for this stop. To do this, use only information needed by people who use that bus stop.

UNIT 1 • Lesson 2    15

## Language Review

**Look at your bus schedule on page 14 again. On your own paper, write two sentences about your bus schedule that use the items below.**

- commas in a series or list
- commas with a city and a state

## Writing

> **WRITING**
>
> Friendly e-mails do not have to be fancy. Just say all that you need to say.
>
> Put a meaningful subject on your e-mail so your reader can find it again easily.

**Answer the items below.**

1. Say that a friend needs information from your bus schedule. Think of one reason your friend needs to use the schedule. Write your reason below.

   _____

   _____

   _____

2. Now write an e-mail to your friend below. First, write your friend's name and a subject where it belongs. Second, write about the part of the schedule that your friend needs to know. Check your e-mail and make any changes.

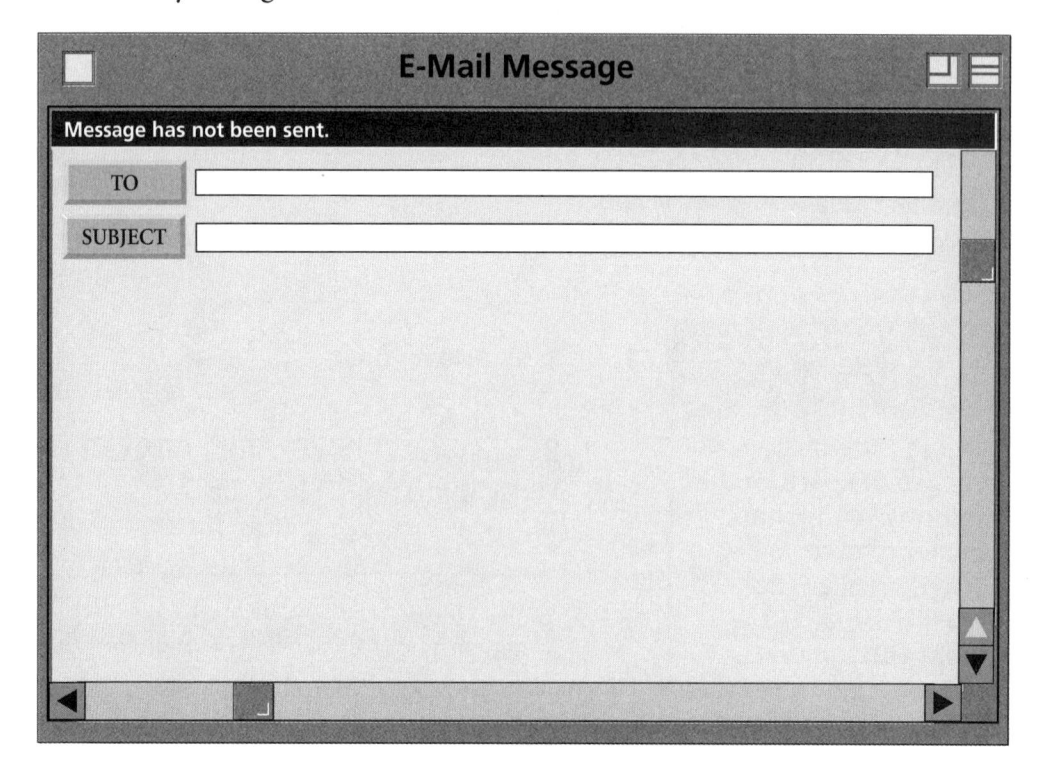

   **E-Mail Message**

   Message has not been sent.

   | TO | |
   | SUBJECT | |

## CAREER

A license to drive a bus is called a Commercial Driver's License (CDL).

To get a CDL, people must follow the laws in their state. First, people need to have:

- a good driving record
- good vision
- good hearing
- normal to fast reaction time

Second, people must pass written tests on:

- general knowledge
- knowledge of passengers
- knowledge of air brakes

Third, people must pass driving tests on:

- bus safety
- bus control
- city street driving
- open-road driving

**Career Connection**

**Read the Career box to the left. Then read about the three people below. Which person do you think could get a Commercial Driver's License? Why or why not?**

1. Alyssa has has been driving for ten years and loves to drive. She has never gotten a ticket. She can read fine print with her glasses. She can hear OK.

   Do you think Alyssa could get a CDL? Circle one.   Yes   No

   Why or why not? _____

   _____

   _____

2. David is a mechanic. He fixes vehicles and knows a lot about them. He has gotten two tickets in the last month. Both times, David said he did not see the stop sign. Other than this, he is a good driver.

   Do you think David could get a CDL? Circle one.   Yes   No

   Why or why not? _____

   _____

   _____

3. Tara sees and hears well. She is not good at fixing things and cannot change a tire. Tara is a safe driver. She has always wanted to drive a school bus.

   Do you think Tara could get a CDL? Circle one.   Yes   No

   Why or why not? _____

   _____

   _____

   _____

# UNIT 2: TELEPHONE BOOKS

## Lesson 3 — BEFORE READING

## Page from the Telephone Book

**PHONICS**

Digraphs are two letters that work together to create a new sound.

Three common digraphs are **ch**, **sh**, and **th**.

### Letters and Sounds

**Use the digraphs sh, th, or ch to complete the words below. The first two have been done for you.**

1. _th_ irst
2. _ch_ alk
3. _____ ird
4. _____ ank
5. _____ art
6. _____ arm
7. _____ ant
8. _____ eft
9. _____ aft
10. _____ elf
11. _____ urn
12. _____ est
13. _____ ift
14. _____ irt
15. _____ rift
16. _____ ild
17. _____ ark
18. _____ ipmunk
19. _____ arp
20. _____ rink
21. _____ orn

**Look at the twenty-one words above. What do all these words have in common? Hint: Look at the last two letters in each word.**

_____

_____

**LIFE SKILLS**

The **white pages** of a telephone book list a person's name, address, and telephone number.

The **yellow pages** list a business's name, address, and telephone number.

### Use What You Know

**Answer the questions below.**

1. What is one way the white pages and yellow pages in a telephone book differ?

   _____

   _____

2. Is your family listed in your local telephone book?  Circle one.   Yes   No

   If yes, write the page number. _____

18   UNIT 2 • Lesson 3

## Lesson 3

### READING  Page from the Telephone Book

Page 276 Telephone Book          WHITE PAGES          MURPHY–MURRAN

**MURPHY** Brian & Kyra
    489 Burr Ave 78227 ...............555-6464
    Christy 7227 Glen Hill 78221....555-5364
    Arletta M 314 E Nate 78226 ......555-8333
    C 422 Zephyr Dr 78229 ..............555-8339
    David 6502 Bander 78228 .........555-6675
    Garvin 610 S Ellison Dr 78225..555-9021
    Hue Knollwood Dr 78223 .........555-1000
    Jason ..............................................555-9222
    Jed & Janie 2015 Fish Trail
        78223...........................................555-9985
    Juan 8622 Starcrest Dr 78230....555-9075
    Larry 6130 Ingram Rd 78229 ....555-3535
    Matt 2224 W Misty 78230 .........555-2322
        Kid's Phone............................555-9995

    Ralph L & Edna 166 Elkins Ave
        78226........................................555-4534
    Tess 7810 Callan St 78229..........555-9426
    Tomas S & Netta 124 Linda Lou Dr
        78223........................................555-3081
    Whit 171 Hermine St 78222......555-7684
    W 19907 Wittenburg Dr 78226.555-9343

**MURR** Cal 546 N Lincoln 78227...555-2301
    Lynn 3421 S Bankey 78220........555-3431
    PT ................................................555-3781

**MURRAN** Mitchell 14 N Rowe
    78221........................................555-3296
    Mitchell ....................................555-3297

**City Zip Code Key**
| | | |
|---|---|---|
| 78220—Campton | 78224—Wilton | 78228—Foster |
| 78221—Brighten | 78225—Belgrade | 78229—Selma |
| 78222—Carroll City | 78226—Irondale | 78230—Roseville |
| 78223—Barrington | 78227—Nolan | |

# Lesson 3

**AFTER READING**

## Pages from the Telephone Book

**STRATEGY**

**Reread** is a reading strategy. Use it to search for and find facts you need.

**READING COMPREHENSION**

Figuring out information helps you understand what you read.

**Reading Comprehension**

**Read the telephone book page on page 19. Then answer the questions below.**

1. **Reread:** Find **Tomas Murphy**. What can you find out from his telephone listing? Write the answers on the lines below.

   Tomas's full name _____

   Wife's name _____

   Street address _____

   City _____

   Zip Code _____

   Telephone number _____

2. **Figure It Out:** How many cities are part of this page? _____

   How do you know? _____

   _____

   _____

3. **Read for Details:** Read the information about Cal Murr. Now write four details below from this telephone book page.

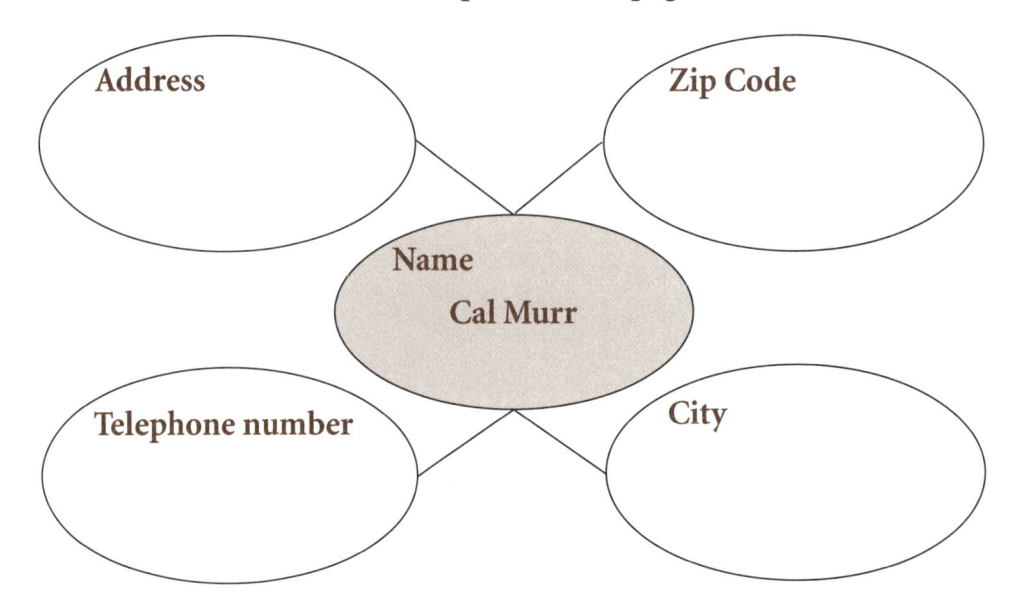

   - Address
   - Zip Code
   - Name: Cal Murr
   - Telephone number
   - City

20   UNIT 2 • Lesson 3

**LIFE SKILLS**

All causes have an effect. Understanding the effects can help you make wise choices.

4. **Cause and Effect:** Some people do not have their name or the telephone number in the telephone book. What are three effects of this choice? One has been done for you.

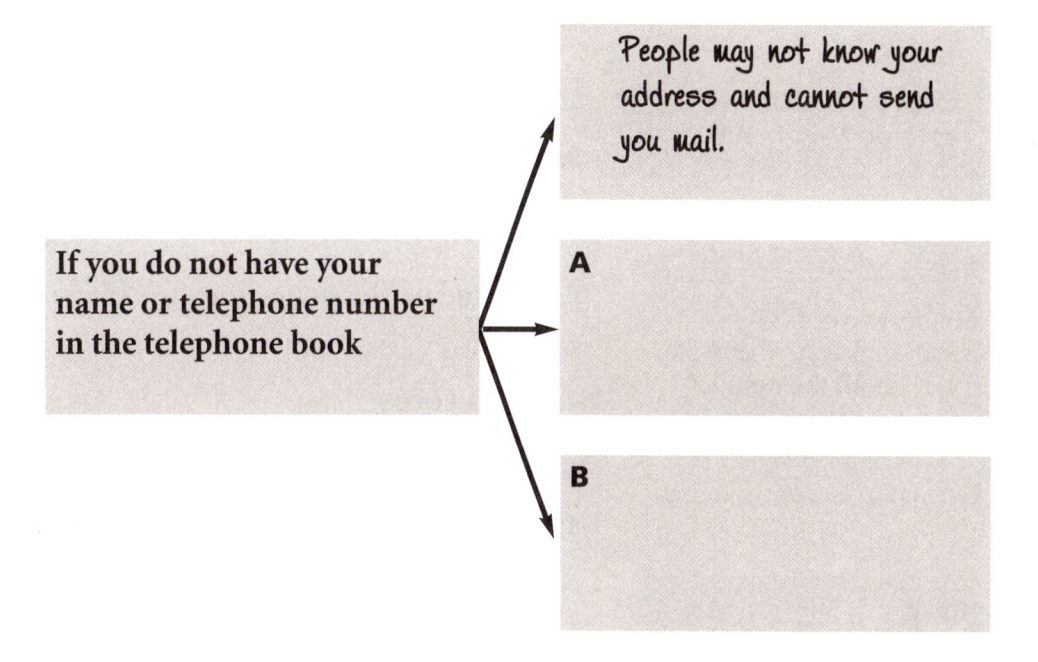

```
                                    → People may not know your
                                       address and cannot send
                                       you mail.

If you do not have your
name or telephone number     →      A
in the telephone book

                                    → B
```

**Letters and Sounds Review**

**Write the words in the box where they belong below. Some words belong in both columns.**

| harp  | sheep | thing | shift | wink  | chunk |
| shiny | chant | think | vent  | cheek | chest |

**Begins with ch, sh, or th**                **Ends with a blend**

_____                      _____
_____                      _____
_____                      _____
_____                      _____
_____                      _____
_____                      _____
_____                      _____

UNIT 2 • Lesson 3   21

## LANGUAGE

A comma is needed between a day and a year.

**Example:** Jared was born on May 1, 1990.

## LIFE SKILLS

Sometimes you have to look at all the details to find out what you want to know.

## LANGUAGE

Some words used in addresses are often abbreviated, or shortened.

**Examples**
**N.** stands for **north**

**Ave.** stands for **avenue**

**Rd.** stands for **road**

**Dr.** stands for **drive**

### Language

**Add the missing commas to the sentences below.**

1. Marsha Kyle and Donna moved to Reno Nevada on April 7 2004.
2. Do David Jessica and Servando all live at the same place?
3. Do you think Tom Narva Joel and Lisa know each other?
4. Do you think Adam was born on June 12 1990?
5. Is Irondale Texas the home of Arletta Leon and Mary?

### Life Skills Focus

**Figure It Out: Now answer the questions below.**

1. Read the Language box to the left. Then write the abbreviation next to the word it stands for below. One has been done for you.

   **A** South ___S._____   **E** East _____
   **B** Drive _____     **F** Street _____
   **C** West _____      **G** North _____
   **D** Road _____      **H** Avenue _____

2. Why do you think telephone books use abbreviations for addresses?

   _____
   _____
   _____

3. Telephone books do not use periods after abbreviations. Why?

   _____
   _____

# Lesson 4

## BEFORE READING

# Your Own Telephone Book Page

**WORD SKILLS**

Follow these patterns to add the **y** suffix:

fun + n + y = funny

luck + y = lucky

whine − e + y = whiny

### Word Skills

Read the words in the box. Add the y suffix to each word. Then write each new word in the sentence where it belongs below.

| juice | wind | cheese | rock | fog |

**1.** I love a sweet, _____ peach.

**2.** I like a thick and _____ pizza.

**3.** It was so _____, we couldn't see 12 feet ahead.

**4.** The tree blew over on a _____ day.

**5.** The yard is too _____ to plant a tree.

### Use What You Know

Tape, staple, or glue a copy of a white page from a telephone book to page 24. Then answer the questions below.

**1.** A person's telephone number or address might be wrong in the local telephone book. How could this happen? Write two reasons below.

**A** _____

_____

**B** _____

_____

**2.** Jane moved to Wilton, Wisconsin a week ago. Will her information be correct in the Wilton telephone book? Circle one.   Yes   No

Why? _____

_____

_____

UNIT 2 • Lesson 4   23

# Lesson 4 READING  Your Own Telephone Book Page

**Make a copy of a white page from a telephone phone book. Tape, staple, or glue the copy to this page.**

# Lesson 4

## AFTER READING

## Your Own Telephone Book Page

### Reading Comprehension

**Read your white page from a telephone book on page 24. Then answer the questions below.**

1. **Reread:** Choose one name from your page. What can you find out from this telephone listing? Write the answers below.

   Full names _____

   Street address _____

   City _____

   Zip Code _____

   Telephone number _____

2. **Figure It Out:** How many cities are in this part of the telephone book?

   _____

   How do you know this? _____

   _____

3. **Read for Details:** Choose a name from page 24. Write the name in the middle circle below. Now write four facts about this person from reading the telephone book page.

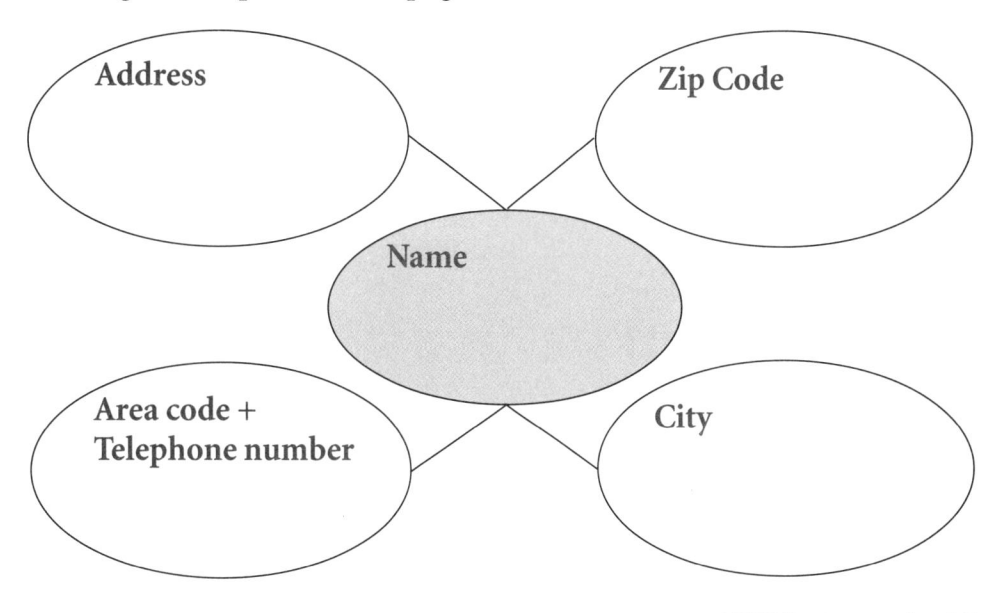

UNIT 2 • Lesson 4   25

**4. Cause and Effect:** Some people list only their first initial and last name in the telephone book. What are two effects of this choice?

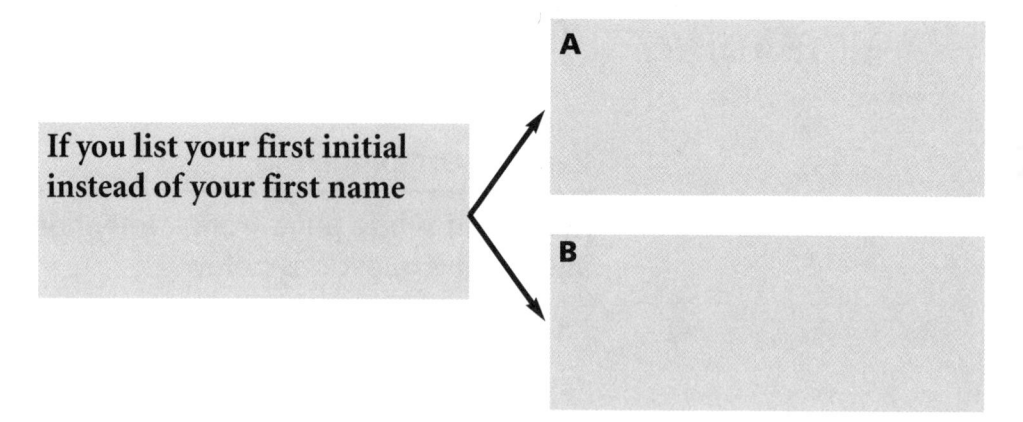

| If you list your first initial instead of your first name | → A |
|---|---|
| | → B |

## Language Review

**Use your own paper to write three sentences about people you know using the items below.**

- a sentence that uses a list
- a sentence that uses a city and a state
- a sentence that uses a date. Write the month, day, and year.

When you are done, check your work. Make any changes.

## Writing

**Choose one name from page 24. On your own paper, write a short story about that person. Write one or two paragraphs. When you are done, proofread. To proofread, check your work and make any changes.**

**Then trade with a classmate and proofread each other's stories. Get your short story back. Make any changes. Write a final story.**

## CAREER

At work, people offer ideas for changes. To come up with good ideas, many people take apart related things or ideas. Then they compare the parts. They look for ways to make the things or ideas better.

**Career Connection**

**Take Apart and Compare: Look over the telephone book pages on pages 19 and 24. Write four things you would change to make these two pages more alike. Then write why you would make each change.**

**1.** I would change _____

_____

because _____

_____

**2.** I would change _____

_____

because _____

_____

**3.** I would change _____

_____

because _____

_____

**4.** I would change _____

_____

because _____

_____

UNIT 2 • Lesson 4    27

# UNIT 3: RECIPES

## Lesson 5 — BEFORE READING: Avocado Dip, Fruit Dump Cake, and Beef Tacos

### PHONICS

Three digraphs, **ch, sh,** and **th,** are often at the beginning and ending of words.

**Examples:** with, cash

Sometimes a third letter is added to an ending digraph, making it a blend **and** digraph.

**Example:** hitch

### VOCABULARY

**garlic**
a strong-tasting herb used in cooking

**microwave**
an oven that cooks food quickly

**parsley**
a leafy herb used for cooking or decoration

**pineapple**
a tropical fruit with spiny leaves, a hard outside, and a sweet inside

**recipe**
the ingredients needed and the instructions to cook something

**tomato**
the red fruit of the tomato plant

### Letters and Sounds

**Read the words in the box. Then write the words where they belong below.**

| such | cherry | stink | chin | thin | chip |
| court | cheese | mash | link | rest | bath |
| park | much | shake | chain | cast | burst |
| dish | rich | push | she | self | math |

**Begins with ch, sh, or th** | **Ends with ch, sh, or th** | **Ends with a blend**

1. _____  9. _____  17. _____
2. _____  10. _____  18. _____
3. _____  11. _____  19. _____
4. _____  12. _____  20. _____
5. _____  13. _____  21. _____
6. _____  14. _____  22. _____
7. _____  15. _____  23. _____
8. _____  16. _____  24. _____

### Use What You Know

1. Read the names of the three recipes below. Which one would you like to eat? Circle your answer.

   Avocado Dip     Fruit Dump Cake     Beef Tacos

2. What do you think are three ingredients in the recipe you circled? Write the ingredients below.

   _____

   _____

   _____

## Lesson 5 READING: Avocado Dip, Fruit Dump Cake, and Beef Tacos

---

**Recipe For:** Avocado Dip
**Recipe From:** Mitch

1 avocado, chopped
2 large tomatoes, chopped
1/4 cup chopped green onion
1 teaspoon chopped garlic
1 tablespoon chopped fresh parsley
1 tablespoon olive oil
1/2 tablespoon lemon juice

In a large bowl, mix all the above together. Serve with corn chips.
Time to Make: 30 minutes.

---

### Cook Notes

- tablespoon—measurement used in cooking equal to 3 teaspoons
- teaspoon—measurement used in cooking equal to $\frac{1}{3}$ tablespoon

---

**Recipe For:** Fruit Dump Cake
**Recipe From:** Mrs. Banning

1 20-ounce can crushed pineapple
1 20-ounce can cherry or apple pie filling
1 package yellow cake mix
1 stick of butter, chopped into small pieces
1/2 cup chopped nuts

Dump the pineapple into the bottom of 9" x 13" cake pan. Top with the pie filling. Toss the yellow cake mix on top and press lightly. Top the cake mix with the butter pieces. Toss nuts on top. Bake 70 minutes at 350° or until golden brown. Time to Make: 30 minutes + baking time.

---

**Recipe For:** Tacos
**Recipe From:** Ann

1 pound ground beef
1 package taco mix
8 soft taco shells
1 medium onion, chopped
2 tomatoes, chopped
4 cups lettuce, chopped
2 cups cheese, chopped
1 cup sour cream

Follow taco mix directions to prepare ground beef and taco mix. Microwave taco shells on high for 30 seconds. Fill each taco shell with taco meat, onion, tomatoes, lettuce, cheese, and sour cream. Eat right away. Time to Make: 25 minutes.

## Lesson 5

**AFTER READING**

# Avocado Dip, Fruit Dump Cake, and Beef Tacos

**READING COMPREHENSION**

Think about any pictures that go with what you are reading. Pictures can help you better understand what you read.

Reading Comprehension

**Read the recipes on page 29. Then answer the questions below.**

1. **Organize Ideas:** Write facts from the recipes into the chart below.

|  | Fresh Ingredients | Chopped Food | Time to Make |
|---|---|---|---|
| Avocado Dip |  |  |  |
| Fruit Dump Cake |  |  |  |
| Beef Tacos |  |  |  |

2. **Group Ideas:** Read the six recipe card files below. Write each recipe name where it belongs.

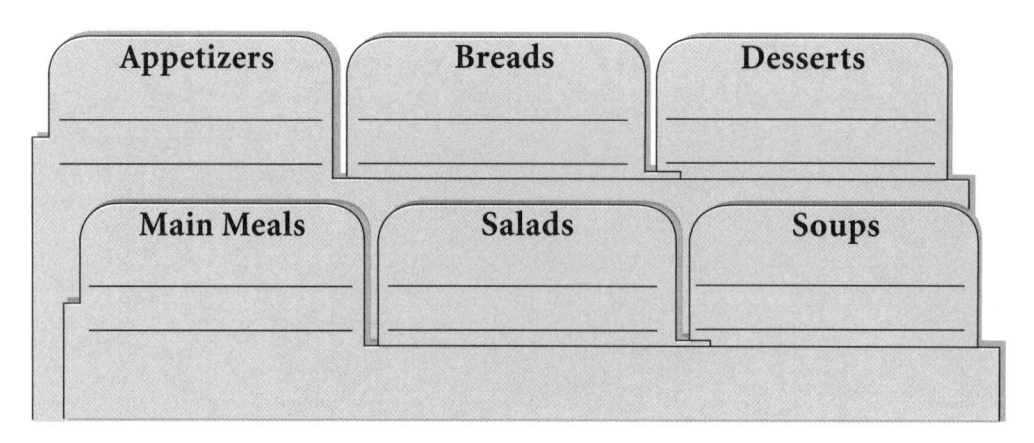

**Appetizers**

**Breads**

**Desserts**

**Main Meals**

**Salads**

**Soups**

3. **Picture It and Make a Picture:** Picture a piece of the baked Fruit Dump Cake. What colors do you see? Do you see the cake as warm or cold? How big is this piece of cake? On your own paper, draw a picture of the piece of cake.

**Letters and Sounds Review**

Use the clues to find and circle the answers. Answers end with a blend, or begin or end with **ch, st,** or **th**. Look for answers up, down, or diagonally. One has been done for you.

Clues
1. Right, not wrong
2. Feeling you have when you need a drink
3. First, second, ___
4. A covered sitting area around a house
5. Mix of ice cream, fruit, and milk
6. Vegetables that are not cooked or frozen
7. Yellow vegetable
8. Dark dessert or candy
9. A type of red-fruit pie
10. Catfish, cod, and perch
11. What ice cream will do in the refrigerator
12. A shape made by the sun

```
y  m  c  x  s  h  a  d  e  w  q
r  c  o  r  r  e  c  t  j  m  m
r  x  r  w  f  i  s  h  p  r  e
e  y  n  n  t  h  i  r  d  t  l
h  r  a  m  s  q  u  i  e  u  t
c  e  a  o  l  h  k  s  q  x  w
f  r  e  s  h  b  a  t  f  y  e
i  c  b  d  u  j  p  k  y  q  l
```

### LANGUAGE

Add commas between:
- the parts of a series. A series is three or more words. **Example:** Raja, Do, and Phil are late.
- a city and a state, and after a state in a sentence. **Example:** Pat lives in Hope, Maine, and plays soccer.
- a day and a year. **Example:** Jordan was born on May 1, 2005.
- the name, street, city, and state of an address in a sentence. **Example:** Tina lives at 11 Huron Street, Lake Elmo, Minnesota.

Do NOT add a comma between a state and zip code.

### Language

**Add the missing commas to the sentences below.**

1. Vegetables such as tomatoes lettuce and peas are good for you.
2. I made my first dump cake on August 8 2000.
3. You can buy great fresh apples in Sharp Michigan.
4. I sent a box of apples to Jon Linder 783 North Fog Avenue Ripton Vermont 05766.
5. Eaton California is known for its great bread jam and butter.
6. I bought a book from The Fun Company 54 Smith Street Homer Illinois 61849.
7. A family in Fork Alaska ate turkey mashed potatoes and peas on March 27 2003.
8. Sarah Brie and Tope moved on June 3 2003.

UNIT 3 • Lesson 5

## LIFE SKILLS

Some people like to share their recipes. To do this, they may write their recipes on recipe cards.

Most recipe cards are 3" × 5" or 4" × 6". Larger recipe cards can be folded to fit into a recipe box.

Good recipes have these parts:
- A title
- The name of the person or place where the recipe came from
- The number of servings the recipe makes
- A list of ingredients
- The order to put the ingredients together
- Directions to cook or bake the dish

Sometimes recipes give ideas about how to serve the dish.

### Life Skills Focus

**Think of a favorite dish that is made in your home. Write the recipe on the recipe card below. Use all the parts listed in the Life Skills box on the left.**

Recipe Title: _____
From: _____ Number of Servings: _____

# Lesson 6

## BEFORE READING

## Your Own Recipe

### Word Skills

**WORD SKILLS**

Follow these patterns to add the suffix **er** or **or**:

hike − e + er = hiker

trot + t + er = trotter

edit + or = editor

bluff + er = bluffer

Read each word below. Then add the suffix er or or. Write the new word where it belongs.

| Word | New Word | Meaning |
|---|---|---|
| 1. race | _____ | —one who races |
| 2. sing | _____ | —one who sings |
| 3. talk | _____ | —one who talks |
| 4. win | _____ | —one who wins |
| 5. advise | _____ | —one who advises |
| 6. dive | _____ | —one who dives |
| 7. grab | _____ | —one who grabs |
| 8. visit | _____ | —one who visits |
| 9. sit | _____ | —one who sits |

### Use What You Know

**Make a copy of a favorite recipe. Use a different recipe than the ones on pages 29 or 32. Tape, staple, or glue the copy to page 34. Then answer the questions below.**

1. Have you ever made this recipe? Circle one.   Yes   No

2. Could you make the dish without looking at the recipe?   Yes   No

3. If you made this recipe but mixed it up a little, do you think it would still taste good?   Yes   No   Why or why not? _____

_____

_____

UNIT 3 • Lesson 6   33

# Lesson 6 READING Your Own Recipe

**Make a copy of a favorite recipe. Use a different recipe than the ones on pages 29 or 32. Tape, staple, or glue your recipe to page 34.**

# Lesson 6 · AFTER READING: Your Own Recipe

**READING COMPREHENSION**

Group things to make sense of what you read.

## Reading Comprehension

**Read your recipe on page 34. Then answer the questions below.**

1. **Organize Ideas:** Work with two classmates. Write information from your three recipes into the chart below.

|  | Fresh Ingredients | Chopped Food | Time to Make |
|---|---|---|---|
| Your Recipe |  |  |  |
| Other Recipe 1 |  |  |  |
| Other Recipe 2 |  |  |  |

2. **Group Ideas:** Read the six recipe card files below. Write each of the three recipes above where it belongs.

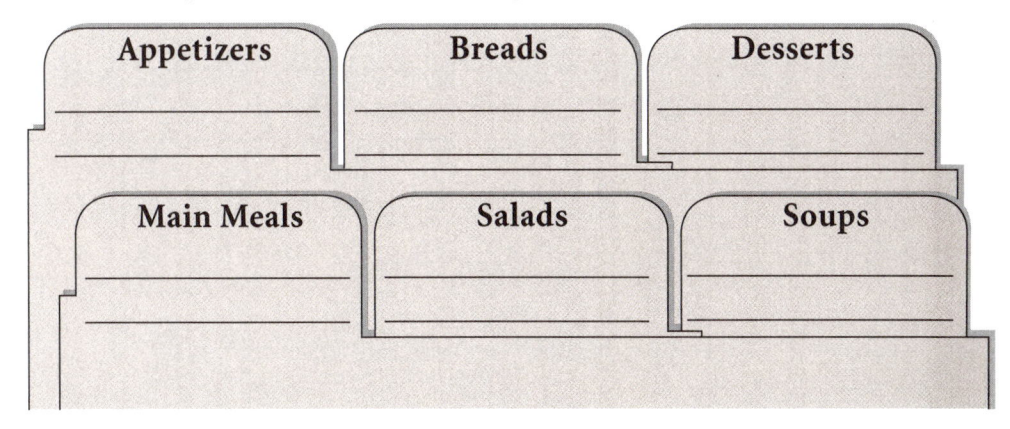

- **Appetizers**
- **Breads**
- **Desserts**
- **Main Meals**
- **Salads**
- **Soups**

3. **Picture It:** Picture how your recipe will look when it is ready to eat. On your own paper, draw a picture of your recipe. Write the recipe name below your picture.

UNIT 3 • Lesson 6   35

## Language Review

**Use your own paper to write three sentences about favorite foods. Use the items below.**

- a sentence with a city and state
- a sentence with a date. Use a month, day, and year.
- a sentence with a complete address

### WRITING

Use your own words to sum up what you have read. It is easier to say what you mean when you use words you know well.

## Writing

**In your own words, write the steps to make your recipe on page 34. Picture making the recipe in your mind. If you need to, rewrite your recipe, but do not copy it. Write about the recipe in your own way. When you are done, read your writing. Make any changes.**

## CAREER

Have you or a family member cooked from a cookbook? Creating cookbooks is a big business.

Companies take these steps to create cookbooks:

- Plan cookbooks so they will sell and make money
- Choose recipes that taste good to many people
- Make sure the recipes work and taste good
- Design cookbooks to look nice
- Write cookbooks so they are easy to use
- Print cookbooks for people
- Be sure people know about the cookbooks and can buy them

**Career Connection**

**Choose one of the steps from the Career box on the left. Circle the step. Now, think about how a cookbook company worker would do that step. Write your ideas below.**

_____
_____
_____
_____
_____
_____
_____
_____
_____
_____
_____
_____
_____
_____
_____
_____

# UNIT 4: Dictionaries

## Lesson 7 BEFORE READING

# Dictionary Page

**PHONICS**

Blends and digraphs such as **ch**, **sh**, and **th** can fall inside words.

**VOCABULARY**

**definition**
the meaning of a word

**dictionary**
a book that lists many or all words in a language, in ABC order

**pronunciation**
how a word is said

### Letters and Sounds

**Read the words in the box. Write the words where they belong below.**

| angry | smoke | share | windy | then | blue |
| ouch | shovel | teeth | event | chew | grin |
| machine | tree | fault | mister | mashed | mother |
| pest | reply | other | foolish | depend | with |

| Begins with a blend | Has a blend inside | Ends with a blend |
|---|---|---|
| 1. _____ | 5. _____ | 9. _____ |
| 2. _____ | 6. _____ | 10. _____ |
| 3. _____ | 7. _____ | 11. _____ |
| 4. _____ | 8. _____ | 12. _____ |

| Begins with ch, sh, th | Has ch, sh, or th inside | Ends with ch, sh, or th |
|---|---|---|
| 13. _____ | 17. _____ | 21. _____ |
| 14. _____ | 18. _____ | 22. _____ |
| 15. _____ | 19. _____ | 23. _____ |
| 16. _____ | 20. _____ | 24. _____ |

### Use What You Know

**Answer the questions below.**

1. Have you ever used a dictionary? Circle one.   Yes   No

2. Dictionaries tell the meanings of words. What are two other things that dictionaries tell?

   _____   _____

3. Why don't people usually read an entire dictionary page at one time?

   _____

   _____

# Lesson 7

## READING   Dictionary Page

*how to pronounce word*

*where the word came from*

*definition or meaning*

**ken•nel** (ken´ l) **1.** *n.* dog house; **2.** *n.* **kennels,** *pl.* place where dogs are kept. *v.* **ken•neled, ken•nel•ing** or **ken•nelled** [**Kennel** comes from a **Latin** word meaning "dog."]

**Ken•tuck•y** (kən tuk´ ē) **1.** *n.* a state in the southern middle part of the U.S. *Short Form:* KY **Capital:** Frankfort [**Kentucky** comes from a **Cherokee** word meaning "land of tomorrow" or "meadow land."]

**kept** (kept) *v.* past forms of **keep**: *I kept the note in my pocket.*

**ker•nel** (kûr´ nl) **1.** *n.* the soft part inside the shell of a nut or inside the seed of a fruit. **2.** *n.* the grain or seed of a plant, such as corn **3.** *n.* the main part of anything.

**ketch•up** (kech´ əp) *n.* sauce to use with meat, fish, potatoes, and other foods. Ketchup is made mostly of tomatoes with other things added. Also spelled **catsup**.

**ket•tle** (ket´ l) **1.** *n.* large pot for cooking; **2.** *n.* teapot

**key** (kē) **1.** *n.* small metal tool to open and close locks and to start cars. **2.** *n.* answer to a puzzle or a problem: *Jared looked at the key to check the answers.* **3.** *adj.* main ones: *The key people are all here.* **4.** *v.* to use computer keys: *Key in the information.* *n. pl.* **keys;** *v.* **keyed, keying**

**Key²** (kē) *n.* **Francis Scott** (fran´ sis), 1779–1843, American writer. Wrote the words to "The Star Spangled Banner."

*a kettle*

### Pronunciation Guide for the **Dictionary**

| | | | | | | | | | |
|---|---|---|---|---|---|---|---|---|---|
| a | act | i | it | oo | book | ch | chief | ə | sound |
| ā | able | ī | ice | o͞o | loot | ng | sing | | a in ago |
| â | dare | o | hot | ou | out | sh | shoe | | e in taken |
| ä | arm | ō | over | u | up | th | thin | | i in pencil |
| e | ebb | ô | order | ū | cute | th | this | | o in lemon |
| ē | even | oi | oil | û | urge | zh | vision | | u in circus |

*parts of speech*

UNIT 4 • Lesson 7   39

## Lesson 7 AFTER READING: Dictionary Page

**STRATEGY**

**Study Pictures** is a reading strategy. You can often find information in pictures.

**READING COMPREHENSION**

Try to use a new word every day. This will grow your knowledge of words.

**CRITICAL THINKING**

Use the **trial and error** tool to remember information. To use this tool, start with one piece of information. Repeat the piece until you remember it. Add a second piece of information. Repeat the two pieces until you remember both. Continue until you have learned all the pieces of information.

### Reading Comprehension

**Read the dictionary page on page 39. Then answer the questions below.**

1. **Study Pictures:** One word has a definition and a picture. Study the picture. Now read the definition. What are two things in the picture that are not in the definition? _____
_____
_____

2. **Think Further:** Look up the word *kernel* in a classroom dictionary. Write the definition below.

    kernel _____
    _____
    _____
    _____
    _____

    Now read the definition of *kernel* on page 39. Do the two dictionaries have the same definitions?   Yes   No

3. **Trial and Error:** Flash cards are a good way to learn information. To make flash cards, write one word from page 39 on a 3" × 5" blank card. On the back of each card, write the first definition of each word. Continue to write the words and their meanings on cards. Then use the cards to learn the words and their meanings.

## READING COMPREHENSION

Some writing can have both facts and opinions. A **fact** is a statement that can be proven true.

**Example of a Fact:** St. Paul is the capitol of Minnesota.

An **opinion** is a statement of belief. Opinions are neither right nor wrong.

**Example of an Opinion:** St. Paul is the best city in Minnesota.

## LIFE SKILLS

A dictionary tells you four things:
- how to say a word
- what the word means
- how the word is used
- where the word came from

**4. Fact or Opinion:** Read the box to the left. Then read the sentences below. Write **F** next to the facts. Write **O** next to the opinions.

A _____ **Kernel** is a hard word to say.

B _____ Words should have no more than two meanings.

C _____ Dictionaries tell how to correctly use words in sentences.

D _____ The chart at the bottom of the dictionary page tells how to say the words.

E _____ **Kenneling** should be its own entry instead of being listed under **kennel**.

F _____ Some words on page 39 come from Latin words.

G _____ The word **kettle** has two meanings.

### Letters and Sounds Review

Read the words in the box. Then write each word where it belongs below. Four words do not belong.

| beach | bathtub | explode | vacation |
| destroy | chin | wink | strong |
| bake | tower | against | bashful |
| trade | eighth | them | several |

**Begins with a blend**    **Has a blend inside**    **Ends with a blend**

1. _____    3. _____    5. _____

2. _____    4. _____    6. _____

**Begins with ch, st, or th**    **Has ch, sh, or th inside**    **Ends with ch, sh, or th**

7. _____    9. _____    11. _____

8. _____    10. _____    12. _____

UNIT 4 • Lesson 7    41

## LANGUAGE

Sometimes a noun is followed by an explanation. However, the sentence means the same without the explanation. Set these explanations apart with commas.

**Example:** Elena, my sister, likes to fish.

## LIFE SKILLS

Dictionaries may look the same, but they all differ in four ways:

- the listed words
- definition of words
- markings that show how to say words
- number of pictures (many, few, or none)

## LIFE SKILLS

Dictionaries meet different needs.

- Little kids need dictionaries with fewer words compared to teens. Teens need more complete dictionaries.
- Companies choose different words for their different dictionaries. A science dictionary has different words than a general dictionary, for example.

### Language

**Read the sentences below. Then add the missing commas.**

1. Bethe my sister's best friend likes to read.
2. She keeps a dictionary a red one close by.
3. I find glossaries small dictionaries in the backs of books helpful.
4. My eyes tired from hours on the computer need to rest.
5. Jorge my father reads a book each week.

### Life Skills Focus

**Alike and Different:** Compare the dictionary page on page 39 with a dictionary in your classroom. How are they different? How are they the same? Write your answers in the chart below.

|  | Dictionary Page on Page 39 | Classroom Dictionary |
|---|---|---|
| Number of words on page |  |  |
| Sample word for the **long i** sound |  |  |
| First definition for the word **kennel** |  |  |
| Number of pictures on a page |  |  |
| Words with suffixes listed in different ways |  |  |
| Use of **bold** and *italics* |  |  |
| Pronunciation of the word **kennel** |  |  |

# Lesson 8 BEFORE READING: Your Own Dictionary Page

### Word Skills

**Read the words before each sentence. Add a suffix from the box below to each word. Then write the new word in the sentence where it belongs.**

| ing | ed | y | er | or |
|---|---|---|---|---|

1. (reply) He _____ just in time.

2. (laugh) Lance _____ at the funny story.

3. (pup, taste) The _____ _____ the shoe.

4. (edit) I want to be an _____ of my school newspaper.

5. (fast, reward) The _____ runners were _____ with a short break.

6. (dip) I'll serve the punch if you will be a _____.

7. (judge, skate) Bart _____ the _____ contest.

8. (operate) The _____ of the dump truck fell asleep.

9. (hop) The coach kept us _____.

10. (luck, wave) Josh is _____ to have _____ hair.

### Use What You Know

**Make a copy of a page from a dictionary. Tape, staple, or glue the copy to page 44. Then answer the questions below.**

1. Have you used this dictionary before? Circle one.   Yes   No
   If yes, why did you use it? _____
   _____

2. Dictionaries are a reference tool. Do you think most people have a dictionary at home?   Yes   No
   Why? _____
   _____

UNIT 4 • Lesson 8   43

# Lesson 8 READING  Your Own Dictionary Page

**Choose a page from a dictionary. Make a copy of the page. Then tape, staple, or glue the copy to this page.**

# Lesson 8

**AFTER READING** Your Own Dictionary Page

### Reading Comprehension

**Read the dictionary page on page 44. Then answer the questions below.**

1. **Study Pictures:** Are there pictures on your dictionary page 44? Circle one.   Yes   No   If yes, what can you can learn from the picture that is not in the definition?

   _____

   If no, why do you think no pictures were used? _____

   _____

   _____

2. **Think Further:** Write two ways you could use a dictionary.

   **A** _____

   **B** _____

3. **Trial and Error:** Choose ten words from page 44. Write each word on a flash card. On the back of each card, write the first two meanings. Then use the cards to learn the meanings of the words.

4. **Fact or Opinion:** Write two facts and two opinions based on page 44.

   Fact 1 _____

   _____

   Fact 2 _____

   _____

   Opinion 1 _____

   _____

   Opinion 2 _____

   _____

UNIT 4 • Lesson 8   45

**Language Review**

**Use your own paper to write three sentences about helpful books. Use the items below.**

- a sentence with a date. Use a month, day, and year.
- a sentence with a complete address
- a sentence with a noun followed by an explanation. The sentence will mean the same without the explanation.

**Writing**

**Look up each word below in a classroom dictionary. Write one definition for each word. Use only the given space. Proofread your work. Make any changes.**

1. rogue _____

2. ration _____

3. tyrant _____

4. double _____

5. junior _____

6. vinegar _____

7. nickname _____

8. include _____

9. scalp _____

10. cooperative _____

---

**WRITING**

Sometimes you have less space to write in than you like. So, you may have to write small. Or you may have to choose your words carefully.

**WRITING**

To proofread, check over your work. Find and fix any mistakes.

## CAREER

Some kinds of jobs are found in many career areas. Some of these common jobs take care of these needs:

- Advertising
- Building needs
- Equipment repairs
- Financial duties
- Food
- Health care
- Main company business
- Office furnishings
- Office supplies
- Outside grounds care
- Printed items for the company
- Sales
- Technical equipment and support
- Training
- Travel

## CAREER

You can find information about jobs from many sources. Here are two ideas:
- Talk to someone who has a job you may like.
- Look at the *Occupational Outlook Handbook* by the federal government. Find this book at your public library or on the Internet at **http://www.bls.gov/oco/**.

## Career Connection

**1.** Think of seven jobs connected with creating dictionaries. Write the jobs below.

### Jobs Connected with Creating Dictionaries

A _____

B _____

C _____

D _____

E _____

F _____

G _____

**2.** Look at your job list above. What two jobs interest you?

_____

_____

**3.** How can you find more information about these jobs?

_____

_____

_____

_____

_____

## Lesson 9: BEFORE READING

**UNIT 5: INDEX**

# Work Sharp Office Products Index

### VOCABULARY

**envelope**
a paper cover in which a letter or something flat can be mailed

**invisible**
cannot be seen

**label**
a tag used to attach information to an item

**tear-proof**
cannot be torn

**videotape**
magnetic tape used to record and play back home videos, television programs, and movies

### Letters and Sounds

Read the clues below. Think of words with the digraphs ch, sh, or th or words with blends. Write the words in the puzzle.

**Across**
1. A school subject
4. Used with "nor"
5. Costly and nice
7. Hurry
9. To make sudsy

**Down**
2. An idea
3. Sun, rain, wind
5. To hook a door
6. Round things that hold food
8. A cut made with glass

### Use What You Know

People who work in offices use many types of supplies. Read the list of office supplies below.

1. Put a check beside each office supply you have used.

   ____ tape             ____ eraser         ____ paper

   ____ scissors         ____ staples        ____ blank CDs

   ____ pencil           ____ paper clip     ____ computer

   ____ telephone        ____ batteries      ____ waste basket

   ____ folders          ____ markers        ____ calendar

2. Read the list of office supplies again. Circle each item you have used at home.

48 UNIT 5 • Lesson 9

# Lesson 9

**READING** Work Sharp Office Products Index

### LIFE SKILLS

An index is a list in ABC order of the items in a book. An index gives the page number where each item can be found.

**PRODUCT INDEX: T-W**

### T

Tacks .....................351
Tape
   General ............272–274
   **Invisible** ...........272–274
   Packaging ..........239–242
   Video ..................896
**Tear-Proof Envelopes** .......55
Telephone Products
   Address Books
   ...............395, 400, 422
   Answering Machines
   ............829, 831, 833–36
   Batteries ........829, 835–36
   Caller ID .......827–828, 833
   Cords ..............828, 829
Telephones ...........843–849
Televisions/VCRs ......754–757
Thumbtacks ..............351
Tough Envelopes ........57, 230
Towels
   Paper ..............477, 478
   Cloth ..................479

Trash Bags ............442–443
Trays
   Coin/Change ............286
   Desktop 686–695, 697, 700, 702
   Drawer ......61, 273, 691, 705
Tubes, Mail ..............237

### V

VCRs/Televisions ......754–757
**Videotape Labels** .......15, 896
Videotapes................896

### W

Wall Calendars
  ..72, 373, 378–385, 1018, 1019
Wall Clocks, See Clocks
Wall Maps ................280
Warning Signs .............460
Wastebaskets
   ...........444–445, 690, 692

**1023** Work Sharp Office Products     *FREE* Next-Business Day Delivery

# Lesson 9 AFTER READING

# Work Sharp Office Products Index

## STRATEGY

Using **Context Clues** is a reading strategy. Use it to learn unknown words. For example, the main headings and subheadings of an index work as context clues for each other.

## LIFE SKILLS

Indexes have **main headings** and **subheadings**. Subheadings always relate to the main headings.

## CRITICAL THINKING

**What It Stands For** is a thinking skill. Use it to look for an item in an index. If you cannot find the item, use other words that mean about the same.

An index sometimes lists items in more than one way. However, an index cannot list every way.

## Reading Comprehension

**Read the index on page 49. Then answer the questions below.**

1. **Context Clues:** Find one subheading for each main heading below. Write the subheadings where they belong in the chart. Then, tell how the main headings and subheadings work as context clues for each other. One has been done for you.

| Main Heading | Subheading | Explain |
|---|---|---|
| Trays | Coin | The words together tell what the type of tray it is |
| Tape | | |
| Towels | | |

2. **Main Idea and Details:** Fill in the missing detail below.

Main Idea: Envelopes

Detail 1: Tough Envelopes

Detail 2:

3. **What It Stands For:** Read the words below. Write one or more words that you could use instead of the words in the four boxes. One has been done for you.

| Trash Bags | Thumbtacks | Clear Tape | Wastebaskets |
|---|---|---|---|
| | | invisible tape | |

50 UNIT 5 • Lesson 9

4. **Author's Purpose:** Circle the four word sets below on page 49. Then explain why the author repeated these word sets in the index.

| | |
|---|---|
| Videotapes | VCRs/Televisions |
| Tape, Video | Televisions/VCRs |

The author repeated these words sets because _____

_____

_____

### Letters and Sounds Review

**On page 49, find six words that fit in the blanks below. Then write the words where they belong.**

| Has a blend | Has ch, sh, or th at the beginning or ending |
|---|---|
| 1. _____ | 4. _____ |
| 2. _____ | 5. _____ |
| 3. _____ | 6. _____ |

### Language

**LANGUAGE**

Commas are needed before every three numerals in a large number.

**Example:** 3,000,000

**LANGUAGE**

Do NOT use a comma between a state and zip code.

### Language

**Add the missing commas to these sentences.**

1. The Work Sharp Products catalog has 1053 pages.

2. The catalog index lists over 14400 items.

3. Baker Box a company that makes boxes spent $1453365 on office supplies last year.

4. Send Baker Box orders to 353 North Wilson Court Jensen Utah 84035.

5. Amanda Collins a buyer for Baker Box signed for $1326345.

6. Lisa Perry the president wondered who had signed for the other $127020. She asked Carlo.

7. Carlo a new buyer said he would find this information.

| LIFE SKILLS |
|---|

ABC order is used in many areas. Here are some examples:

- Class lists
- Dictionaries
- Encyclopedias
- Lists at work
- Name tags at an event
- Time cards at work
- White pages of a telephone book
- Yellow pages of a telephone book

**Life Skills Focus**

**ABC Order: Number these office supplies into ABC order.**

**1.** Number the items from 1–12, with 1 being the word closest to A.

_____ paper

_____ envelopes

_____ trash bags

_____ clocks

_____ address labels

_____ glue

_____ rubber bands

_____ boxes

_____ files

_____ markers

_____ ruler

_____ desk lamp

**2.** Write 5 more office supplies below.

_____

_____

_____

_____

_____

**3.** Draw a line from each office supply you just wrote to where it fits in Item 1 above.

# Lesson 10 BEFORE READING: Your Own Index

**WORD SKILLS**

A **prefix** is a word part added to the beginning of a word.

Below are three prefixes and their meanings.

**un**—not, opposite of
**re**—again
**mis**—bad or wrong

## Word Skills

**Read the word before each sentence. Add the prefix un, re, or mis to each word. Write the new words where they belong.**

1. (lucky) The number 3 is _____ for my aunt.

2. (wanted) Sore throats are _____ at our house.

3. (speak) It's all right to _____. Just don't try to hide it.

4. (do) _____ all mistakes on your report before you give it to your teacher.

5. (guided) You are _____. You can't go into work late a lot and still keep your job.

6. (paint) Let's _____ the walls next week.

7. (new) _____ your library book. Then you can keep it another three weeks.

8. (design) Please help me _____ this poster.

9. (important) Let's not fight about _____ things.

10. (behaving) It is sometimes tough to talk to _____ children.

## Use What You Know

**Make a copy of a page from an index. You can find indexes in books, catalogs, and some magazines. Tape, staple, or glue your copy to page 54. Then answer the questions below.**

1. Have you used the index on page 54? Circle one.   Yes   No

2. What is one reason you would use this index? _____

_____

_____

UNIT 5 • Lesson 10

## Lesson 10 READING Your Own Index

Make a copy of a page from an index. You can find indexes in some books, magazines, and catalogs. Then tape, staple, or glue your copy to this page.

*Lesson* **10 AFTER READING** Your Own Index

**Reading Comprehension**

**Read your index page on page 54. Then answer the questions below.**

1. **Context Clues:** Choose two main headings and subheadings from your index. Write the headings and subheadings below. Tell how they work as context clues for each other.

| Main Heading | Subheading | How They Work as Context Clues |
|---|---|---|
|  |  |  |
|  |  |  |

2. **Main Idea and Details:** Write a main idea and two details from page 54 in the boxes below.

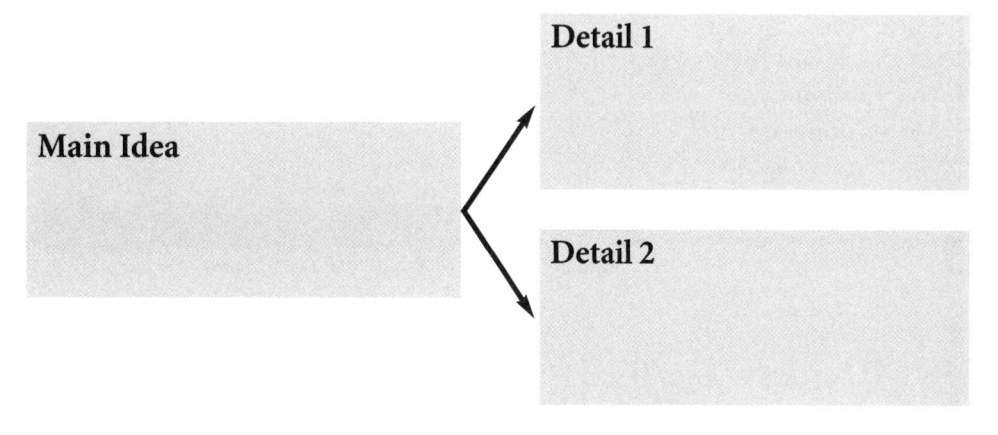

Main Idea → Detail 1

Main Idea → Detail 2

3. **What It Stands For:** Find three words from your own index page that are hard for you to read or understand. Write the words below. Now think of another word or words that mean the same thing as the words you wrote. Write these new words where they belong below.

**Words Hard to Read or Understand**

_____   _____   _____

**Words that Mean About the Same**

_____   _____   _____

UNIT 5 • Lesson 10   55

**4. Author's Purpose:** Would the index on page 54 help you use the book?
Yes   No

Why or why not? _____

_____

_____

_____

## Language Review

**Use your own paper, write three sentences about office products that use the items below.**

- a complete address
- a restatement of a noun
- numbers that need commas

## WRITING

Use your journal to write your thoughts freely. Write about what you are learning. This can help you better understand what you read and learn.

## Writing

**Start a journal about learning to read better. To get started, look through pages 8 through 57 of this book. Read the boxes on the pages. Choose two or more helpful tips. In your own words, write why they are helpful to you. Proofread your writing. Make any changes.**

### CAREER

It is important to like your job. If not, you may not be happy. People who do not like their jobs may want to look for different jobs.

### Career Connection

**Below are some jobs that have to do with office supplies. Do you think you would like any of these jobs? Put a check in the Yes or No box.**

| Jobs | Yes ✔ | No ✔ |
|---|---|---|
| **1. Buyer:** Orders products for a company | | |
| **2. Writer:** Writes the information in sales pieces and on product labels | | |
| **3. Designer:** Designs labels and sales pieces | | |
| **4. Salesperson:** Sells office products to companies | | |
| **5. Clerk:** Sells office supply products in a store | | |
| **6. Bidder:** Figures out how much to charge for large orders | | |
| **7. Ad Person:** Plans how to advertise office products | | |
| **8. Cleaning Person:** Cleans the store after hours | | |
| **9. Factory Worker:** Puts together many different products | | |
| **10. Truck Driver:** Drives the products to companies around the country | | |

UNIT 5 • Lesson 10

## Lesson 11 BEFORE READING

### UNIT 6: TABLES OF CONTENTS

# Make Your Own Crafts Table of Contents

### PHONICS

A **hard c** or **g** comes at the end of a word or is followed by an **a, o, u,** or a constant.

Examples: came, go big

A **soft c** or **g** often is followed by an **e, i,** or **y**.

Examples: cell, gym, race

### Letters and Sounds

**Read the words in the box below. Then write each word in one of the six boxes where it belongs.**

| English city giant | fishing nice picnic | egg coffee softly | gate age Richie | crime ago peace | magic darkness mother |
|---|---|---|---|---|---|

**Has ch, sh, or th inside**

1. _____
2. _____
3. _____

**Has a blend inside**

4. _____
5. _____
6. _____

**Has a soft c**

7. _____
8. _____
9. _____

**Has a hard c**

10. _____
11. _____
12. _____

**Has a soft g**

13. _____
14. _____
15. _____

**Has a hard g**

16. _____
17. _____
18. _____

### Use What You Know

**Answer the questions below.**

1. Have you ever received a homemade gift?  Circle one.   Yes   No
   If yes, what was the gift? _____

2. Have you ever given anyone a gift that you made?   Yes   No
   If yes, what was it? _____

   Did you enjoy making the gift?   Yes   No

3. Say that a friend's birthday is next month. What gift could you make for your friend? _____

### VOCABULARY

**bookmark**
a piece of material used to mark one's place in a book

**denim**
a tough cotton fabric often used in jeans

**fleece**
a soft, heavy fabric used for clothing

**frilly**
decorative

**plaid**
fabric with a pattern of unevenly spaced repeated stripes that cross

**trinket**
a small ornament, piece of jewelry, or keepsake

# Lesson 11

**READING** *Make Your Own Crafts* Table of Contents

## Table of Contents

*Make Your Own Crafts* is a book with 100 fun crafts to make as great gifts for friends and family. The crafts are grouped into eight interest areas.

**INTEREST AREA 1**
Gifts for Teen Girls

| | |
|---|---|
| **Trinket** Box | 1 |
| Clip-On Cell Phone Holder | 3 |
| Framed Poem | 5 |
| Blossom **Bookmarks** | 7 |
| Flower Petal Frame | 9 |
| **Frilly** Lace Pillows | 11 |
| Necklace Lipstick Case | 13 |
| Flower Basket | 15 |
| Giant Photo Board | 17 |
| Striped Lunch Bag | 19 |
| Paperback Book Cover | 21 |
| Picture Key Chain | 23 |
| Fancy Gift Tags | 25 |
| Beaded Bracelet | 27 |
| Wooden Trinket Box | 29 |
| Butterflies Wind Chimes | 31 |

**INTEREST AREA 2**
Gifts for Teen Boys

| | |
|---|---|
| **Denim** Pillows | 33 |
| Paperback Book Cover | 35 |
| Money Clip | 37 |
| Tiger Key Chain | 39 |
| Shirt with Pocket | 41 |
| Pen Box | 43 |
| Family Picture Frame | 45 |
| CD Holder | 47 |
| **Fleece** Hat | 49 |
| Sports Bookmarks | 51 |
| TV Treat Pack | 53 |
| Auto Mirror Hanger | 55 |
| School File Holder | 57 |
| Address Book | 59 |
| Scarf with School Colors | 61 |
| **Plaid** Photo Album | 63 |

# Lesson 11 AFTER READING

## *Make Your Own Crafts* Table of Contents

### STRATEGY

**Sum It Up** is a helpful reading strategy. To sum up, put ideas into your own words. You understand information better when it is in your own words.

### READING COMPREHENSION

Try to conclude and connect when you read. That way, you add your own thoughts to what you read. Your reading becomes more personal. Then you are more likely to remember and understand what you read.

### CRITICAL THINKING

Write down all ideas when you brainstorm. Then look through your ideas and choose the best ones.

**Reading Comprehension**

**Read the Crafts-By-You Table of Contents on page 59. Then answer the questions below.**

1. **Sum It Up:** Tell about the types of crafts in this catalog. Write two or three sentences. _____

   _____

   _____

   _____

   _____

2. **Solve This:** Choose three crafts on page 59. On your own paper, draw what you think each finished craft would look like.

3. **Make Connections:** Write the names of three people you give gifts to below. Choose a gift for each person from page 59. Write the gift next to the person's name.

   | | Name | Gift from Page 59 |
   |---|---|---|
   | A | _____ | _____ |
   | B | _____ | _____ |
   | C | _____ | _____ |

4. **Brainstorm:** Say that you wanted to give some gifts, but you do not have much money. What are four things often thrown away that could be used to make gifts? Write your ideas below.

### LIFE SKILLS

The table of contents includes the title and beginning page number of each section of a book.

## Letters and Sounds Review

**Read the clues below. Think of words with soft cs and gs. Write the words in the puzzle.**

**Across**
1. Wear on your belt so people can reach you
3. Very sad, overwhelming
6. More than enough
7. Directions for cooking something
9. If you push the ___, you will hang up.

**Down**
2. In the last little while
4. A basement
5. To thrill someone
8. The middle

### LANGUAGE

Add commas before and after the name of a person being spoken to in a sentence.

**Examples:**
- Al, water the plants.
- Be sure, Alix, to walk the dog.

## Language

**Add the missing commas to these sentences.**

1. I like homemade gifts Tam because I get something unusual.

2. Am I talking to Matt the owner of a homemade keychain?

3. Is your house filled with about 64524343 special things?

4. I didn't mean it like that Lora.

5. I've tried to make carmel 1000 times. It always hardens too fast.

6. Lucas maybe you need to make a different homemade gift. What about cookies?

7. What's so special Maggie about a batch of cookies? Anyone can make them.

8. That's not true Lucas. My dad makes cookies that are as hard as rocks.

UNIT 6 • Lesson 11   61

## LIFE SKILLS

Companies go through many steps to plan a new product. Organizing is one of the first steps.

Think of the *Make Your Own Crafts* book on page 59. The book planners first chose the gift areas. Then they brainstormed gifts in each area. They created a table of contents of the gift areas and gifts. They followed the table of contents to create the book.

## LIFE SKILLS

You can find table of contents in books, magazines, newspapers, and on web pages.

### Life Skills Focus

**Organize Ideas:** Think of three other interest areas for the *Make Your Own Crafts* book on page 59. Write each interest in a box below. Then write three crafts for each interest area.

**Interest Area 3**

_____

1. _____
2. _____
3. _____

**Interest Area 4**

_____

1. _____
2. _____
3. _____

**Interest Area 5**

_____

1. _____
2. _____
3. _____

# Lesson 12 BEFORE READING

## Your Own Table of Contents

### WORD SKILLS

Two common suffixes are **ly** and **ful**. They add these meanings:

**ly**—in a way that is
**ful**—full of

### WORD SKILLS

If you don't know which suffix to add, say the word aloud, quietly. You may be able to hear the correct suffix. Or, look the word up in a dictionary.

### Word Skills

Add the suffix **ly** or **ful** to each word below. Write each new word where it belongs. The first one has been done for you. The spelling of some words may change. If needed, use a dictionary.

1. hurt____hurtful____
2. help_____
3. taste_____
4. second_____
5. proud_____
6. thank_____
7. cheer_____
8. happy_____
9. close_____
10. hand_____
11. important_____
12. truth_____
13. spoon_____
14. delight_____
15. last_____
16. glad_____
17. use_____
18. blind_____
19. ear_____
20. play_____
21. correct_____
22. cup_____
23. eager_____
24. hill_____

### Use What You Know

Make a copy of a table of contents from a book. Tape, staple, or glue the copy to page 64. Then answer the questions below.

1. What is the title of your book? _____

2. Have you read this book? Circle one.   Yes   No

3. Why do you think having a table of contents in a book is a good idea?

_____

_____

UNIT 6 • Lesson 12

# Lesson 12 READING   Your Own Table of Contents

**Make a copy of a table of contents from a book. Tape, staple, or glue the copy to this page.**

# Lesson 12 AFTER READING

## Your Own Table of Contents

**READING COMPREHENSION**

Table of contents can tell you:
- What the book is about
- How information in the book is organized
- Where to find information in the book

**Reading Comprehension**

**Read the table of contents on page 64. Then answer the questions below.**

1. **Sum It Up:** What do you think your book is about? Write two or three sentences. _____

_____

_____

_____

_____

2. **Solve This:** After reading the table of contents, do you want to read this book? Circle one.   Yes   No

    Why or why not? _____

_____

_____

3. **Organize Ideas:** How is this book organized? _____

_____

_____

4. **Brainstorm:** Think about the table of contents for your book. Based on the table of contents, write two different titles for the book.

    Title 1 _____

_____

    Title 2 _____

_____

UNIT 6 • Lesson 12   65

## Language Review

**On your own paper, write three sentences about books using the items below.**

- an explanation of the noun
- large numbers that need commas
- names of people being spoken to

## Writing

**The sentences below are in passive voice. Rewrite them in active voice.**

1. The craft was made by Linda.

2. The gift was enjoyed by Nada and Thu.

3. It has been a long time since Julio was seen by me.

4. It has been decided by Joe to make the keychain.

5. The carrots were quickly eaten by the rabbit.

---

### WRITING

In active writing, the subject does the action. Active writing is also called active voice.

Writing that is not active is called passive voice.

**Active:** Clay ran a good race.

**Passive:** A good race was run by Clay.

## Career Connection

**Look at your table of contents on page 64. Then fill in the job map below. These jobs are connected to making books.**

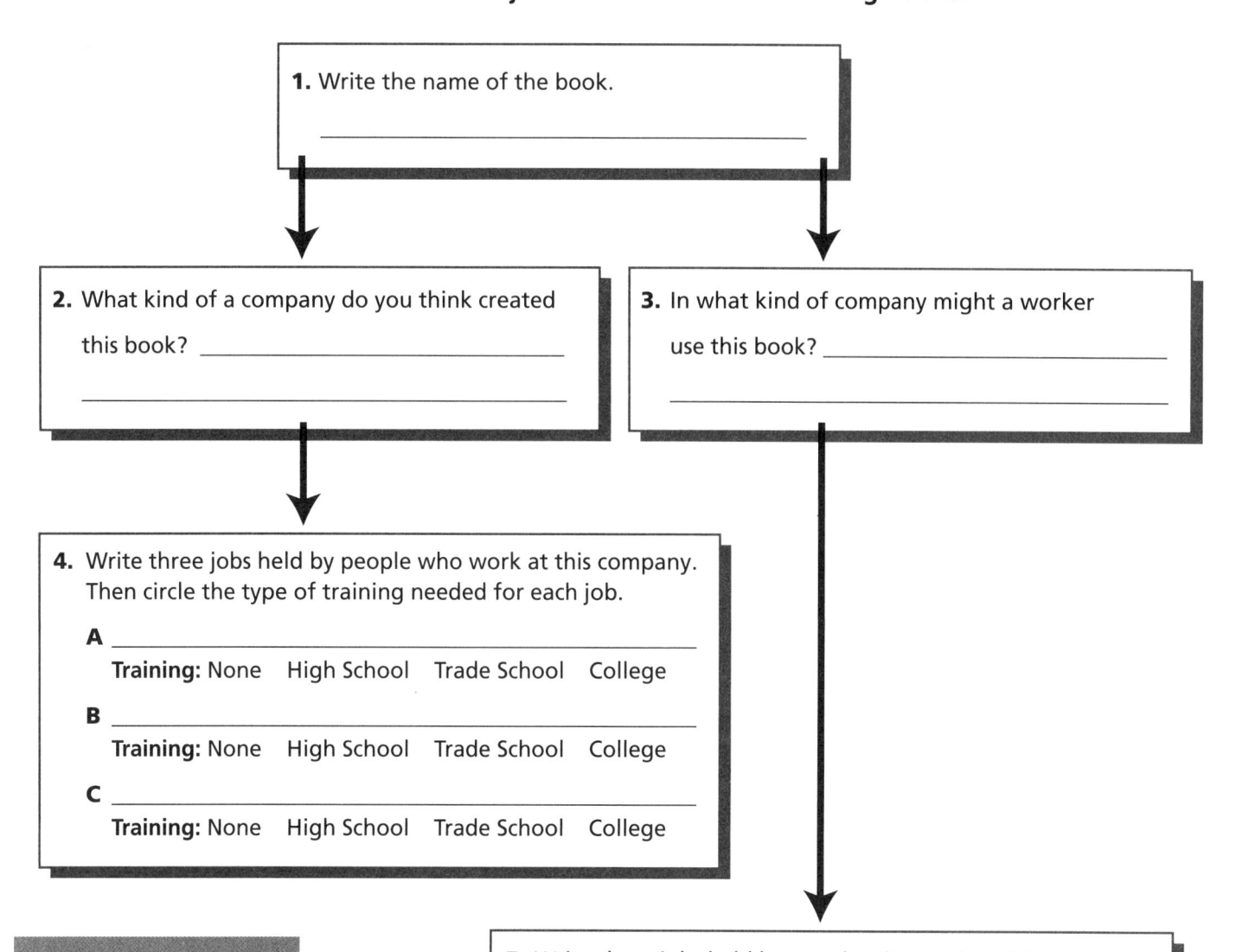

**1.** Write the name of the book.
_____

**2.** What kind of a company do you think created this book? _____

**3.** In what kind of company might a worker use this book? _____

**4.** Write three jobs held by people who work at this company. Then circle the type of training needed for each job.

  A _____
  **Training:** None   High School   Trade School   College

  B _____
  **Training:** None   High School   Trade School   College

  C _____
  **Training:** None   High School   Trade School   College

**CAREER**

Many people work in the book publishing business in the United States.

**5.** Write three jobs held by people who work at this company. Then circle the type of training needed for each job.

  A _____
  **Training:** None   High School   Trade School   College

  B _____
  **Training:** None   High School   Trade School   College

  C _____
  **Training:** None   High School   Trade School   College

## UNIT 7: MOVIE SCHEDULES

*Lesson* **13** **BEFORE READING**

# North Ring Theaters

### PHONICS

Below are three common silent letter pairs. The slashed letter is silent in each pair.

g/h/ as in ghost
f/t/ as in often
i/s/ as in island

### Letters and Sounds

**Read the words in the box. Then write each word in the chart where it belongs below.**

| dislodge | aisle | ghost | mislead | island |
|---|---|---|---|---|
| often | sift | after | hoghouse | soften |
| egghead | dislike | foghorn | | |

g/h/

1. _____

f/t/

2. _____
3. _____

i/s/l

4. _____
5. _____

gh

6. _____
7. _____
8. _____

ft

9. _____
10. _____

isl

11. _____
12. _____
13. _____

### VOCABULARY

**attention**
careful thinking

**audience**
a group of listeners or viewers

**certificate**
a piece of paper that can be exchanged for something else

**general**
for everyone

**guidance**
direction

**online**
on the Internet

**theater**
a place where movies are shown; a movie theater

### Use What You Know

**Answer the questions below.**

1. Write the name of a movie theater in your area. _____
   _____

2. Most theaters belong to a larger group of theaters. Is your theater part of a larger group of theaters? Circle one.   Yes   No   Don't Know

3. Why are most theaters part of a larger group of theaters?
   _____
   _____

68   UNIT 7 • Lesson 13

# Lesson 13

**READING**  North Ring Theaters

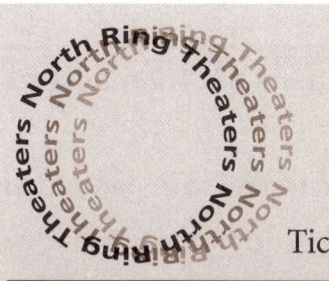

## North Ring Theaters
### 800-555-2335

Tickets **online** at www.northring.com
Gift **Certificates** at box office

Tickets—$9.00      Bargain price before 6:00—$5.00

---

### Bunk Road Theaters
### 1313 North Bunk Road

**Annie's Son** (PG–13)
(11:55  2:30  5:00)
7:30  10:00

**Big Dance** (R)
(12:50  2:50  5:15)
7:50  10:15

**Call Mikie** (PG–13)
(3:10)  7:00  10:35

**Clay's Mystery** (G)
(11:50  2:35  5:10)
7:40  10:10

**Drums & Trumpets** (PG)
(11:30  12:00  2:10
2:40  4:50  5:20)
8:00  10:05  10:30

**High Noon** (R)
(11:15  1:45  4:45)
7:10  9:40

**Long Walk Home** (G)
(1:15  3:30  4:45)

**Maria's Neighbors** (G)
(2:15  5:45)  8:15

**The Reader** (PG–13)
9:00  11:30

**Talking Walls** (R)
7:40  9:10  11:40

### Old Mill Theaters
### 8353 North Old Mill Road

**Amazing Toys** (G)
(11:50  1:40  3:50  5:20)
7:00

**Annie's Son** (PG–13)
(12:55  2:55  6:00)
8:00  10:30

**Anyone's Guess** (R)
(1:50  4:50)  8:15  10:50

**Call Mikie** (PG–13)
(4:10)  7:30

**Clay's Mystery** (G)
(11:05  1:25  3:30  5:25)
7:40  10:10

**Drums & Trumpets** (PG)
(11:10  11:40  1:50
2:20  4:30  5:00)
8:00  10:05  10:30

**High Noon** (R)
(11:15  1:45  4:15)
7:10  9:40

**Long Walk Home** (G)
(12:35  3:10  4:45)

**Maria's Neighbors** (G)
(2:15  4:15 )  6:15  8:15

**The Reader** (PG–13)
4:00  5:30  7:00  8:30

### Festival Screens
### 97 Withers Avenue

**History of the Old West** (G)
All Screens: 7:00  8:20  9:45

---

### Movie Ratings

G — General Audiences. For all ages

PG — Parental **Guidance** Suggested

PG–13 — Parental **Attention** Needed. OK for age 13 and up.

R — 17 and over

# Lesson 13 AFTER READING

## North Ring Theaters

### STRATEGY

**Make It Clear** is a reading strategy. To make something clear, find pieces of connected text. This helps you understand what you read.

### READING COMPREHENSION

Sometimes you must figure out something from what you have read. The reading piece may not say what you need to know.

### READING COMPREHENSION

Charts show information in a visual way. Sometimes information in a chart is easier to understand than just reading the words.

### Reading Comprehension

**Read the movie schedule on page 69. Then answer the questions below.**

1. **Make It Clear:** Some movie times are in parenthesis, such as (11:50  1:40). Why? _____
   _____

2. **Figure It Out:** What are two movies young children may like?

   A _____

   B _____

3. **Read for Details:** Darl, age 16, lives near the two theaters. She wants to see an afternoon movie and be home by 6:00. She can get to a movie by 2:30. What are five movie choices for Darl?

   _____
   _____
   _____

4. **Make a Chart:** Write the five movie titles from Item 3 in the chart below. Then write the movie times for each movie title. One has been done for you.

### Movie Times

| Movie Title | Bunk Road Theaters | Old Mill Theaters |
|---|---|---|
| 1. Long Walk Home | 3:30 | 3:10 |
| 2. | | |
| 3. | | |
| 4. | | |
| 5. | | |

**Letters and Sounds Review**

Read the words in the box. Then write each word in the sentence where it belongs below.

| ghost | drifter | island |
|-------|---------|--------|
| often | dislikes | soften |
| aisle | mislead | |

1. Betty won't eat bananas. She _____ banana bread.

2. Josh's Shop _____ hires high school students.

3. The bride floated down the _____ in her lovely dress.

4. I don't want to _____ you with wrong information.

5. A _____ walked slowly down the highway.

6. Martina was scared! She thought she saw a _____.

7. Have you seen the _____ of Hawaii?

8. I use sheets in the dryer to _____ my clothes.

**Language**

Add the missing commas to these sentences.

1. Over 350000 people saw the *Drifter* during its opening week.

2. *High Noon* a terrible movie is a waste of time.

3. Micah did you know Heather Wang made only $1000000 in that movie?

4. Let's go Carl. The theater ran out of popcorn!

5. Dan did you hear that *Maria's Neighbors* cost $2000000 to make?

6. We got out out of the movie at 9:00 15 minutes early.

## LIFE SKILLS

You make choices about how to spend your free time. So, if you want to see movies, pick ones you are most likely to enjoy. Read movie reviews. Talk to people who have seen movies you want to see.

**Life Skills Focus**

**Look at the Pieces:** Read the eight types of movies below. Put the movie types in the order that you like them. To do this, number them 1–8, with 1 as your favorite. Then write two movie titles next to each movie type.

____ Love Story _____

____ Mystery _____

____ Scary _____

____ Action _____

____ Adventure _____

____ Drama _____

____ Musical _____

____ Comedy _____

# Lesson 14 BEFORE READING

## Your Own Movie Schedules

### WORD SKILLS

Here are four common suffixes and their meaning.

**est**—most
nice − e + est = nicest

✧ ✧ ✧

**ish**—of, like, or being
pink + ish = pinkish

✧ ✧ ✧

**ist**—one who
piano − o + ist
= pianist

✧ ✧ ✧

**ship**—state of, rank, or skill
relation + ship
= relationship

### Word Skills

Read the words in Box A below. Add a suffix from Box B to each word in Box A. Write the new words in the sentences where they belong below.

| A | Words | | | B | Suffixes |
|---|---|---|---|---|---|
| | piano | owner | motor | | est |
| | hot | messy | sad | | ist |
| | pink | child | hard | | ish |
| | | | | | ship |

1. Jolene dislikes playing the piano. She will never be a great _____.

2. The plant had _____ leaves, not reddish leaves.

3. Marcus felt _____. The _____ had no cold air blowing into his car.

4. Kyle bought a house. Because of his _____ of the house, Kyle wants it clean.

5. Her car stopped running. Then she broke her leg. It was the _____ day in her life.

6. Mel's peach was juicy and was the _____. Tom's peach was not ripe, so it was the _____.

7. That's not an adult way to act. That's _____.

### Use What You Know

Find a local movie schedule in a newspaper. Tape, staple, or glue the movie schedule to page 74. Now answer the questions below.

1. Where did you find your local movie schedule? _____

2. What is another place you could find local movie schedules?

_____

UNIT 7 • Lesson 14   73

## Lesson 14 READING  Your Own Movie Schedules

**Find a local movie schedule in a newspaper or on the Internet. Tape, staple, or glue the movie schedule to this page.**

# Lesson 14 AFTER READING

## Your Own Movie Schedules

**CRITICAL THINKING**

Putting information in another form can help make facts more clear.

### Reading Comprehension

**Read the movie schedule on page 74. Then answer the questions below.**

1. **Make It Clear:** Do you see any movies that are early in the day and cost less? Circle one.  Yes   No   How do you know? _____
_____

2. **Understand:** Do you see two movies for young children?   Yes   No

   If yes, write two titles. _____
_____

3. **Read for Details:** Say that you want to go to an afternoon movie and be home by 6:00. The earliest you can get to the movie is 2:30. The movies are all about two hours long. Look at the two theaters closest to where you live. What are three movies you could see?

_____

_____

_____

4. **Make a Chart:** Write the three movie titles above in the chart below. Then write the theater names and the movie times for each movie title.

| Movie Title | Theater Name and Show Time |
|---|---|
| **A** | |
| **B** | |
| **C** | |

UNIT 7 • Lesson 14

**Language Review**

**On your own paper, write three sentences about movies that use the items below.**

- numbers that need commas
- a name of a person being spoken to
- an explanation of the noun

After you finish, proofread your sentences. Make any changes.

**Writing**

**Write a short story about a movie title from page 69 or 74. To get started, choose a movie title. Write it in the circle below. Now brainstorm ideas and write them beside the story lines. If needed, add more idea lines.**

**Put your ideas into a story. On your own paper, write your story. Tell your story so it would work for a movie. When you are done, proofread your story. Make any changes. Write a final story.**

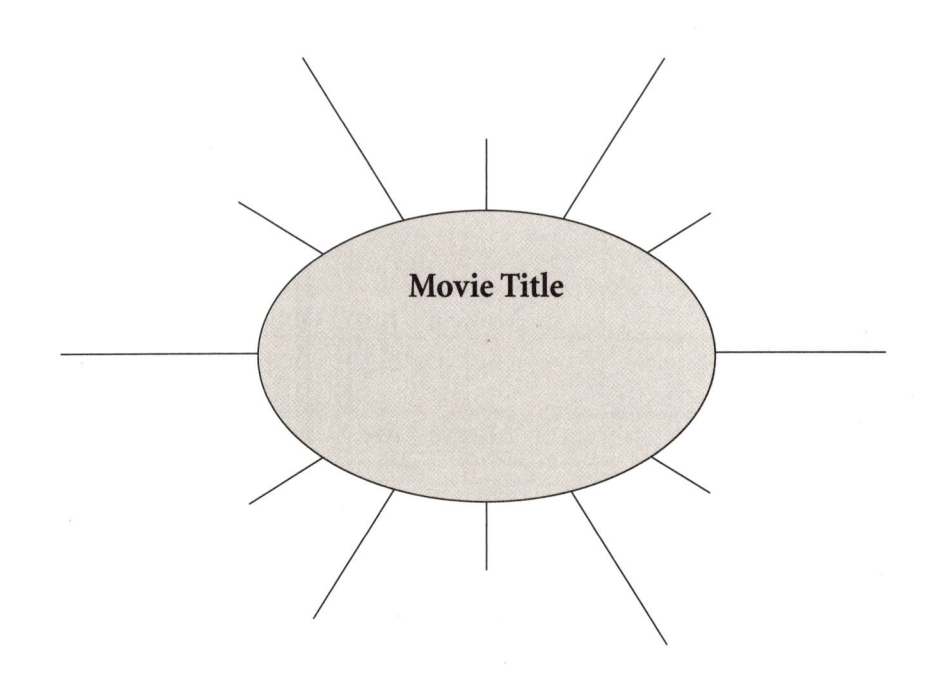

### WRITING

Sometimes it is hard to begin writing a story. One helpful writing tool is a web of ideas for your story.

To start, draw a circle. Write the story title in the circle. Now draw lines coming from the circle. These are your idea lines.

Brainstorm ideas and write them beside the idea lines. Then organize your ideas on another piece of paper. Now use your ideas to begin writing.

*Movie Title*

**CAREER**

Watch and listen to people as they work. This can help you learn about different jobs.

Career Connection

**Think of everyone who works in a movie theater. If it helps, picture a movie theater in your mind.**

1. Write five job titles in the chart below. Then complete the rest of the chart.

| Job Title | Job Tasks | Work Hours | Clothes for Work |
|---|---|---|---|
| A | | | |
| B | | | |
| C | | | |
| D | | | |
| E | | | |

2. Would you like to work in a movie theater? Circle one.   Yes   No

   Why or why not? _____

   _____

   _____

   _____

   _____

UNIT 7 • Lesson 14

**UNIT 8: PACKING SLIPS**

## Lesson 15 BEFORE READING

# Owls Computer Company

### PHONICS

Below are three common silent letter pairs. In each pair, the slashed letter is silent.

/lk as in walk
/lm as in palm
/mn as in autumn

### VOCABULARY

**bill**
charge

**cartridge**
a case or container that holds a substance like ink

**credit card**
a card used to pay for goods or services

**credit**
borrowed money with the promise to pay it back

**customer**
someone who buys goods or services

**deluxe**
luxurious, elegant, or expensive

**invoice**
a list of goods shipped and their prices

**packing slip**
a list of the contents of a package and their prices

### Letters and Sounds

Read the words in the box. Then write the words where they belong below.

| isle | disloyal | soft | column |
| often | mislay | milk | elk |
| elm | raft | caulk | film |
| soften | aisle | bigheart | penmanship |
| chalk | solemn | calm | spaghetti |

**Words with Silent Letters**        **Words Without Silent Letters**

_____  _____        _____  _____

_____  _____        _____  _____

_____  _____        _____  _____

_____  _____        _____  _____

_____  _____        _____  _____

### Use What You Know

**Answer the questions below.**

1. Have you ever seen a packing slip? Circle one.   Yes   No

2. Why do you think some companies use a both packing slip and a bill?

   _____

   _____

3. Color is sometimes added to make important points stand out as you read. Why is this a good idea?

   _____

   _____

## Lesson 15 READING   Owls Computer Company

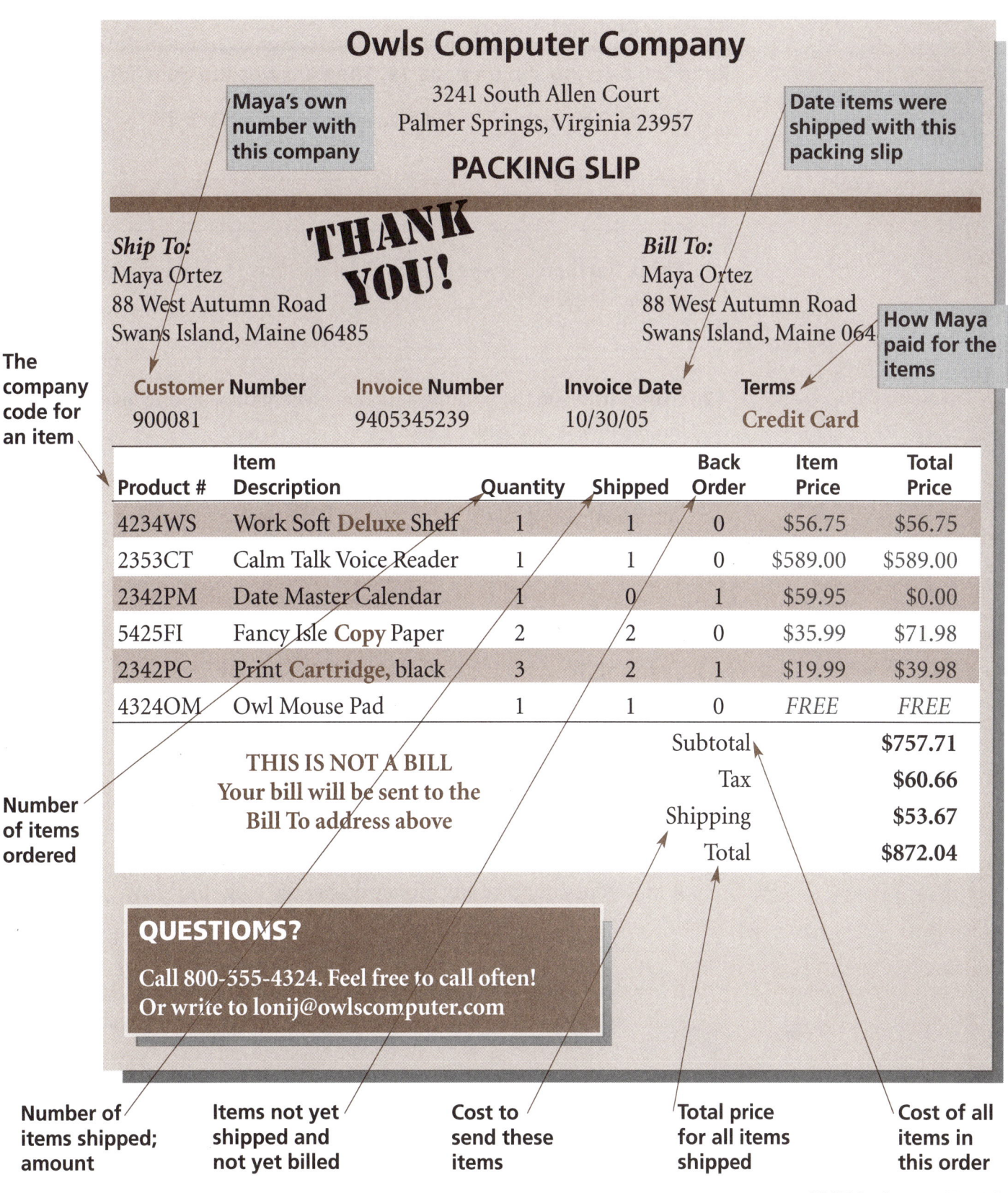

# Owls Computer Company

3241 South Allen Court
Palmer Springs, Virginia 23957

## PACKING SLIP

*Maya's own number with this company*

*Date items were shipped with this packing slip*

**THANK YOU!**

*Ship To:*
Maya Ortez
88 West Autumn Road
Swans Island, Maine 06485

*Bill To:*
Maya Ortez
88 West Autumn Road
Swans Island, Maine 0648

*How Maya paid for the items*

*The company code for an item*

| Customer Number | Invoice Number | Invoice Date | Terms |
|---|---|---|---|
| 900081 | 9405345239 | 10/30/05 | Credit Card |

| Product # | Item Description | Quantity | Shipped | Back Order | Item Price | Total Price |
|---|---|---|---|---|---|---|
| 4234WS | Work Soft Deluxe Shelf | 1 | 1 | 0 | $56.75 | $56.75 |
| 2353CT | Calm Talk Voice Reader | 1 | 1 | 0 | $589.00 | $589.00 |
| 2342PM | Date Master Calendar | 1 | 0 | 1 | $59.95 | $0.00 |
| 5425FI | Fancy Isle Copy Paper | 2 | 2 | 0 | $35.99 | $71.98 |
| 2342PC | Print Cartridge, black | 3 | 2 | 1 | $19.99 | $39.98 |
| 4324OM | Owl Mouse Pad | 1 | 1 | 0 | FREE | FREE |
|  |  |  |  | Subtotal | | $757.71 |
|  | THIS IS NOT A BILL |  |  | Tax | | $60.66 |
|  | Your bill will be sent to the Bill To address above |  |  | Shipping | | $53.67 |
|  |  |  |  | Total | | $872.04 |

*Number of items ordered*

### QUESTIONS?

Call 800-555-4324. Feel free to call often!
Or write to lonij@owlscomputer.com

*Number of items shipped; amount*

*Items not yet shipped and not yet billed*

*Cost to send these items*

*Total price for all items shipped*

*Cost of all items in this order*

UNIT 8 • Lesson 15   79

# Lesson 15 AFTER READING: Owls Computer Company

### Reading Comprehension

**Read the packing slip on page 79. Then answer the questions below.**

1. **Reread:** The Item Price and Total are grayed out. Why? _____

   _____

2. **Think Further:** Tell one reason Maya may have bought the items on the packing slip. _____

   _____

3. **Group It:** Write the packing slip items where they belong below. One has been done for you.

   | Items Maya can use now | Items Maya has to wait for |
   |---|---|
   | Work Soft Deluxe Shelf | Date Master Calendar |

4. **Cause and Effect:** Answer the questions below.

   **A** Maya does not owe any money on her packing slip. Why? _____

   _____

   **B** Maya has called 800-555-4324 to ask about her back orders. However, she gave the wrong customer number. What do you think will happen?

   _____

80   UNIT 8 • Lesson 15

## Letters and Sounds Review

**Find one word on page 79 with each silent letter set below. Write each word below.**

| f̸t | is̸l | l̸k | l̸m | m̸n |

1. _____    4. _____

2. _____    5. _____

3. _____

## Language

**Read the sentences below. Circle the correct words to match the subject and verb.**

1. My order (is, are) late.

2. The items usually (comes, come) five days after I (order, orders) them.

3. The order takers (ask, asks) for the needed information.

4. They (give, gives) you a telephone number to call if you have questions.

5. Customers (has, have) to know what they want before they (call, calls).

6. Sometimes a packing slip (do, does) not show the costs.

7. You must pay if the packing slip says "(Pay, Pays) from this invoice."

8. You may have to (sign, signs) for a package that comes to your house.

9. When I'm not home, the mail person (leaves, leave) packages by the door.

10. Call the company before you (return, returns) something.

---

### LANGUAGE

Sometimes a sentence does not sound right. That's because the subject and verb number may not agree.

A subject or verb can be:

- one—dog, walks
- more than one—dogs, walk

You can often hear if a sentence sounds right. Sometimes, problems are easier to hear if you read the sentences aloud.

Below are two examples. Read them aloud, quietly.

**Do not match:**
- The dog walk with me in the morning.
- The dogs is here.

**Match:**
- The dog walks with me in the morning.
- The dogs are here.

UNIT 8 • Lesson 15   81

## LIFE SKILLS

Companies store the items they sell in warehouses. Warehouses are large rooms or buildings with lots of shelves. Items are stored on shelves.

Warehouses are busy places. Warehouse workers fill, package, and send orders. They also check new items in and put them away.

**Life Skills Focus**

**Picture It:** Read the box on the left. Then picture a warehouse that stores the items on the packing slip on page 79. What does this warehouse look like? Draw a picture below.

82   UNIT 8 • Lesson 15

# Lesson 16 BEFORE READING

## Your Own Packing Slip

**READING COMPREHENSION**

Packing slips and other forms use different features to add meaning. They may use:

- boxes
- bold letters
- underlining
- letter sizes that vary
- color

### Word Skills

**Add a prefix or suffix from the box to each word below. Write the new word beside it. Then use each new word in a sentence.**

| mis | re | un | est | ful | ish | ist | ly | ship |

**1.** visit, _____

_____

_____

**2.** friend, _____

_____

_____

**3.** happy, _____

_____

_____

**4.** style, _____

_____

_____

### Use What You Know

**Find a packing slip. Cover any personal information and make a copy. Tape, staple, or glue the copy to page 84. Then answer the questions below.**

**1.** Look at your packing slip, but do not read it. Put a check next to each feature you see.

____ boxes  ____ underlining  ____ **bold letters**

____ color  ____ letter sizes that vary

**2.** Find the words **Packing Slip** or **Packing List**. Why are these words near the top of the form?_____

_____

UNIT 8 • Lesson 16

# Lesson 16 READING  Your Own Packing Slip

**Find a packing slip. Cover any personal information and make a copy. Tape, staple, or glue the copy to this page.**

Lesson 16 **AFTER READING** Your Own Packing Slip

**READING COMPREHENSION**

Every packing slip is different. Reread the packing slip if something does not make sense. Or, read ahead to figure out something you do not understand.

**Reading Comprehension**

**Read the packing slip on page 84. Then answer the questions below.**

1. **Reread or Read Ahead:** Write one thing on the packing slip you do not understand.

   _____

   Now reread or read ahead on the packing slip. Did this help?   Yes   No

2. **Think Further:** Write two reasons why someone might buy the things on the packing slip.

   _____

   _____

3. **Group Ideas:** Think of two groups to sort the items on the packing list into. Write the title of each group below. Then write the items where they belong. For help, see page 80, item 3.

   |   |   |
   |---|---|
   |   |   |

4. **Cause and Effect:** Complete the sentences below.

   **A** No one was home when an order came to my house, so

   _____

   **B** An order was sent to the wrong address, so

   _____

UNIT 8 • Lesson 16   85

## Language Review

**Read the words below. Use each one in a sentence. Be sure the subjects and verbs agree so the sentences sound right.**

1. (is) _____

2. (are) _____

3. (write) _____

4. (writes) _____

5. (run) _____

6. (runs) _____

## Writing

**WRITING**

Be exact when you write facts. One wrong letter or number could be confusing.

**Say that one item on the packing slip was not sent. However, it is not marked as a back order. Write the information you need to get the item sent to you. Proofread your work. Make any changes.**

_____

_____

_____

_____

_____

_____

### CAREER

Companies give a product code to each item they sell. A product code is made up of numbers and letters. Each number and letter means something. The people at the company use the codes to do their work.

**Career Connection**

**Answer the questions below.**

1. Look at the product codes on the packing slip on page 79. What do the letters in the codes mean?

   _____

   _____

2. Say you are selling a type of shoes. Make a plan for product codes for the shoes. Then write three sample codes below.

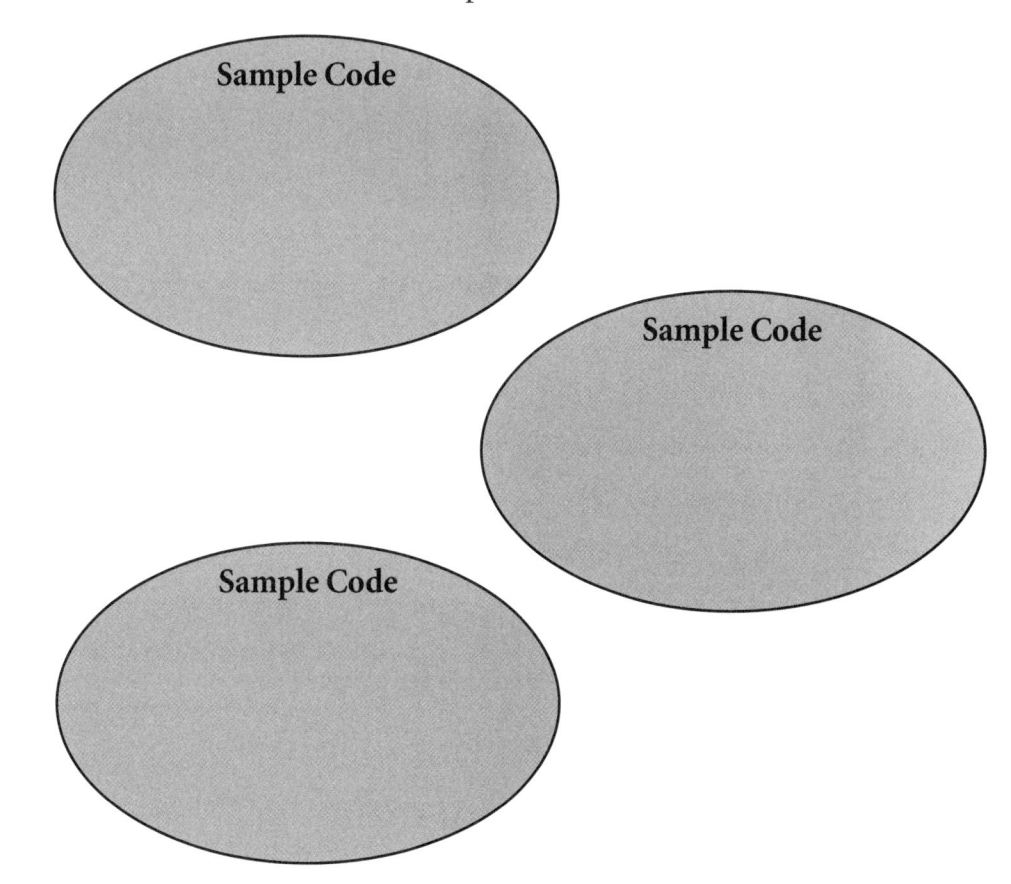

   *Sample Code*

   *Sample Code*

   *Sample Code*

   Why did you use the numbers or letters for your codes?

   _____

   _____

   _____

UNIT 8 • Lesson 16

# UNIT 9: BANK STATEMENTS

## Lesson 17 BEFORE READING
### Checking Account Statement

### PHONICS

Below are two common silent letter pairs. The slashed letter in each pair is silent.

s̸t as in listen
sw̸ as in sword

### VOCABULARY

**check**
a written order directing a bank to pay money

**checking account**
money in a bank that can be taken out by writing a check

**deposit**
money put into a bank account

**period**
a length of time

**statement**
monthly summary from a bank that shows recent deposits, withdrawals, and other information

**withdrawal**
money taken out of a bank account

### Letters and Sounds

Read the words in the box. Then write the words where they belong below.

| island    | stop      | boost    | autumn   | yolk   |
| swordfish | silk      | listen   | beeswax  | soften |
| castle    | answer    | sword    | chimney  | sister |
| swift     | spaghetti | doghouse | busily   | sweet  |

**Words with Silent Letters**             **Words Without Silent Letters**

_____  _____                          _____  _____

_____  _____                          _____  _____

_____  _____                          _____  _____

_____  _____                          _____  _____

### Use What You Know

Answer the questions below.

1. Do you have a checking account? Circle one   Yes   No

2. Why would someone have a checking account? _____
   _____

3. People with a checking account get a statement from their bank each month. What two things can you find out by reading a bank statement?

   A _____

   B _____

88   UNIT 9 • Lesson 17

# Lesson 17
## READING  Checking Account Statement

**West River Bank**
5464 North Carol Street
Forest, Rhode Island 24551
www.riverbank.com
1-800-555-3943

**STATEMENT DATE**
10-01-04

**Account Number**
234525533

**Customer**
Donna T. Lapin
643 South Walton Street
Forest, Rhode Island 24551

**Questions?**
Call 1-800-555-3943.
Report any problems with
your account within 14 days.

WEST RIVER **CHECKING ACCOUNT** Account Number 234525533

### ACCOUNT SUMMARY     Statement Period: 08/14/2004 to 09/15/2004

| Balance Forward | Number of Deposits | Deposits This Period | Number of Withdrawals | Withdrawals This Period | Closing Balance |
|---|---|---|---|---|---|
| 324.95 | 2 | 410.90 | 10 | 285.97 | 449.88 |

### CHECKS AND OTHER WITHDRAWALS

| Date | Check # | Amount | Date | Check # | Amount |
|---|---|---|---|---|---|
| 08/17 | 4811 | 23.75 | 08/29 | 4816 | 33.21 |
| 08/19 | 4812 | 45.73 | 09/06 | 4818* | 12.42 |
| 08/21 | check card | 52.32 | 09/06 | 4819 | 30.10 |
| 08/24 | 4813 | 15.86 | 09/08 | New Checks | 30.00 |
| 08/25 | 4815* | 32.58 | 09/11 | Service Fee | 10.00 |

### DEPOSITS

| Date | Deposit # | Amount | Date | Deposit # | Amount |
|---|---|---|---|---|---|
| 08/20 | 6434 | 321.45 | 08/30 | 5643 | 89.45 |

* check was skipped

page 1 of 1

UNIT 9 • Lesson 17   89

# Lesson 17 AFTER READING

## Checking Account Statement

**Reading Comprehension**

**Read the checking account statement on page 89. Then answer the questions below.**

1. **Author's Purpose:** Why are two check numbers followed by an asterisk (*)? _____
   _____

2. **Organize Ideas:** What list is first on the statement: checks or deposits?
   _____

   Why do you think the statement is organized this way?
   _____

3. **Fact or Opinion:** Read the sentences below. Then write **F** next to the facts. Write **O** next to the opinions.

   ___ Donna spends too much money.

   ___ Donna wrote more than eight checks.

   ___ Donna wrote too many checks.

   ___ It is easy to find information on the bank statement.

4. **Look at the Pieces:** Answer the questions below.

   **A** What is West River Bank's Web site address?
   _____

   **B** What number would Donna call if she has a question about her statement? _____

   **C** To answer the question, the clerk must look up Donna's account information. What number will the clerk use to look up Donna's account?
   _____

## Letters and Sounds Review

**Read the clues below. Think of words with silent letters. Write the words in the puzzle.**

**Across**
2. A bride walks down the _____
5. Plant that hurts
6. Used on a chalkboard
8. Do we have messages on the _____ machine?
9. Did you read the advice _____?
10. A _____ writer secretly writes for famous people.

**Down**
1. To clasp
3. The hard frozen bread dough is _____ in the refrigerator
4. Inside of a hand
6. The city will _____ the old building and tear it down
7. A fancy _____ hangs next to the coat of armor
11. To speak

## LANGUAGE

Verb tense tells when the action in the sentence takes place.

**Present tense** means the action is taking place now. Below are two sentences in present tense.

- I like apples.
- Liu plays flute in the school band.

## Language

**Read the sentences below. Then circle the correct word to make each sentence present tense.**

1. Donna (got, gets) her checking account statement in the mail.
2. Donna always (checks, will check) her statement to make sure it is right.
3. The bank (sends, sent) Daren's statement on the 15th of each month.
4. The bank (prepares, prepared) bank statements on different days.
5. That way, all the bank work (didn't, doesn't) have to be done at once.
6. Jorge moves this week. Before he moves, Jorge (will give, gives) his new address to the bank.
7. Jorge (wrote, writes) checks two or three times a week.
8. Some people (write, will write) more checks than Jorge does.
9. Ben (deposited, deposits) money about once a week.

UNIT 9 • Lesson 17    91

## LIFE SKILLS

Some people use a register to track their checking account deposits and withdrawals. They use this form to record deposits, withdrawals, and account balances.

Each deposit or withdrawal is recorded on a register. A deposit is added to the previous balance. A payment is subtracted from the previous balance. The resulting answer is called the new balance.

It is a good idea for people to compare their register with their bank statement each month.

### Life Skills Focus

**Order:** Donna has missed putting six pieces of information into her check register. The missing pieces are circled. Read page 89 to find the missing information. Then write the missing information where it belongs.

| Number | Date | Description of Transaction | Payment/Debit (-) | Code | Fee | Deposit/Credit (+) | Balance 324.95 |
|---|---|---|---|---|---|---|---|
| 4811 | 8/17 | Aurands Store | 23.75 | | | | 301.20 |
| 4812 | 8/19 | Miner Mail Order | 45.73 | | | | 255.47 |
| | | Books | | | | | |
| | 8/20 | Deposit | | | | 321.45 | 576.92 |
| | | paycheck | | | | | |
| | 8/21 | Check Card | 52.32 | | | | 524.60 |
| 4813 | 8/24 | U.S. Postal Service | 15.86 | | | | 508.74 |
| | | stamps | | | | | |
| 4814 | 8/24 | Movie Time | 13.05 | | | | 495.69 |
| 4815 | ◯ | Metro BW | 32.58 | | | | 463.11 |
| | | Bus Pass | | | | | |
| 4816 | 8/29 | Home Foods | ◯ | | | | 429.90 |
| | | party snacks | | | | | |
| 4817 | 9/2 | The Green Thumb | 10.59 | | | | 419.31 |
| | | flowers | | | | | |
| 4818 | 9/16 | Jay's Stop | 12.42 | | | | 406.89 |
| | | gas | | | | | |
| | 8/30 | ◯ | | | | 89.45 | 496.34 |
| | | from Rady | | | | | |
| 4819 | 9/6 | Edwardo's | 30.10 | | | | 466.24 |
| | | 2 shirts | | | | | |
| | 9/8 | ◯ | 30.00 | | | | 436.24 |
| ◯ | 9/11 | Service Fee | ◯ | | | | 426.24 |
| | | | | | | | |
| | | | | | | | |
| | | | | | | | |

92  UNIT 9 • Lesson 17

## Lesson 18 BEFORE READING: Your Own Bank Statement

### Word Skills

Add one prefix or one suffix from the box to each word below. Use each prefix or suffix once. On your own paper, write a sentence that uses each new word.

| mis | un | er | ful | ish | ly | y |
|---|---|---|---|---|---|---|
| re | ed | est | ing | ist | or | ship |

1. _____ understand _____
2. _____ easy _____
3. _____ fool _____
4. _____ luck _____
5. _____ likely _____
6. _____ nice _____
7. _____ member _____
8. _____ arrange _____
9. _____ laugh _____
10. _____ type _____
11. _____ educate _____
12. _____ beauty _____
13. _____ large _____
14. _____ flip _____

### Use What You Know

Find a bank statement for a checking account. Bank statements are private, so cover the person's name and account number. Make a copy of the statement. Then tape, staple, or glue the copy to page 94. Answer the questions below.

1. Write two ways to spend checking account money for services. Look at page 89 if you need ideas.

   _____   _____

2. What section lists where money was taken from the checking account?

   _____

   _____

UNIT 9 • Lesson 18

# Lesson 18 READING Your Own Bank Statement

**Find a bank statement for a checking account. Bank statements are private, so cover the person's name and account number. Make a copy of the statement. Then tape, staple, or glue the copy to this page.**

## Lesson 18 AFTER READING: Your Own Bank Statement

### Reading Comprehension

**Read the bank statement on page 94. Then answer the questions below.**

1. **Author's Purpose:** Is the bank statement divided into parts?   Yes   No

   Why or why not? _____

   _____

2. **Organize Ideas:** Did any checks not come to the bank?   Yes   No

   How can you tell? _____

   _____

   _____

3. **Fact or Opinion:** Write two facts and two opinions based on the bank statement.

   Fact 1 _____

   _____

   Fact 2 _____

   _____

   Opinion 1 _____

   _____

   Opinion 2 _____

   _____

4. **Look at the Pieces:** Answer the questions below.

   **A** Does the bank give a Web address on the statement?   Yes   No

   If yes, what is it? _____

   **B** What should someone do with a question about the statement?

   _____

UNIT 9 • Lesson 18   95

**Language Review**

**Read each set of verbs below. Circle the verb that is present tense. Then write a sentence that uses each circled verb. Be sure the subjects and verbs agree so that the sentences sound right.**

1. (gives, gave, will give) _____

2. (laughed, laugh, will laugh) _____

3. (sings, sang, will sing) _____

4. (will teach, taught, teach) _____

5. (saves, will save, saved) _____

6. (watched, watch, will watch) _____

### WRITING

To explain why and how about something:
- include all important facts
- get the facts correct
- give the facts in order
- be clear

## Writing

**Why do you think banks send out bank statements? Write your answer below. When you are done, proofread your work. Make any changes.**

_____

**CAREER**

People who work in banks follow proof-of-honesty rules. These rules are in place because bank workers handle lots of money.

Career Connection

**Read the Career box on the left. Then answer the questions below.**

1. **Bank tellers** deal with customers and money. Tellers must prove that the money they took in and out is correct at the end of each day. Why?

   _____
   _____
   _____

2. **Lock box workers** open bank boxes for customers. Customers store important papers and other things in bank boxes. Each bank box needs two keys. The lock box worker has one key and the customer has a second key. Why are both keys needed to open a bank box?

   _____
   _____
   _____

3. **Bank auditors** check bank records often. They make sure different records agree. Why?

   _____
   _____
   _____

4. **Loan officers** approve bank loans to customers. However, loan officers must have their loans approved by others. Why?

   _____
   _____
   _____

# UNIT 10: TV SCHEDULES

## Lesson 19 BEFORE READING

## Tuesday Evening

### VOCABULARY

**cartoon**
a motion picture made up of a series of drawings put on tape or computer that seem to move when seen on television

**crusade**
a strong movement against something wrong or in favor of a new idea

**memory**
events that are remembered

**national**
of a nation, belonging to a whole nation

**professional**
making a business of something

**reptile**
one of a group of cold blooded animals such as snakes, lizards, turtles, alligators, and crocodiles

**tournament**
a contest between people

**wrestle**
to try to throw or force someone to the ground

### Letters and Sounds

Write three words with a silent letter in each box below. For word ideas, look through this worktext or use a dictionary.

| gh | ft | isl |
|---|---|---|
|  |  |  |

| lk | lm | mn |
|---|---|---|
|  |  |  |

| st | sw |
|---|---|
|  |  |

### Use What You Know

**Answer the questions below.**

1. How many hours a week do you watch TV? _____

2. How do you know when TV shows you like will be on? _____
   _____

3. Look at the TV schedule on page 99. What are two things you see right away?
   _____
   _____

98   UNIT 10 • Lesson 19

# Lesson 19

**READING**  Tuesday Evening

## Tuesday Evening — February 18, 2003

[Pay channels shaded. R—Rerun. Movie Key: TVY—All children; TVY7—For children 7 and up; TVG—All Viewers; TV14—Parental Attention Needed; TV14—Parents strongly cautioned; TVMA—Mature audiences only. Ratings from **** (excellent) to * (poor)]

| Time | Channel 15 | Channel 19 | Channel 23 | Channel 25 | Channel 29 | Channel 33 |
|---|---|---|---|---|---|---|
| 6 | 6:00 **Build Your Pet a Home: Birds** | 6:00 **Movie: Pete's Travels** TVG **** Pete has surprises on a trip. | 6:00 **Doctor Rady** R | 6:00 **Legal Cases** R | 6:00 ▲ **Tournament Golf** | 6:00 **The Bill Blue Show** |
| 7 | 7:30 **Build Your Pet a Home: Reptiles** | | 7:00 **Adam Feather** R | 7:00 **The Judge and Bill** | 7:00 **Wrestling Review** | 7:00 **Talking with Brittany** |
| 8 | | 8:00 **Movie: Loni's Song** TV14 *** Loni goes on a **crusade** to save someone dear. | 8:00 **Heroes Cartoons** R | 8:00 **Denver Police** R | | 8:00 **Justin and Friends** |
| 9 | 9:00 **National Dog Show** | | 9:00 **Adam Feather** R | 9:00 **You and Your Money** R | 9:00 **Professional Football Memories** | 9:00 **Did You Say That?** |
| 10 | | 10:00 **Movie: Rover's Friends** TVG ** A boy and his dog make new friends. | 10:00 **Doctor Rady** R | 10:00 **Family Law** R | 10:00 **College Basketball Greats: Where Are They Now?** R | 10:00 **All Friends Here** |
| 11 | | | 11:00 **Madison Memorial** R | 11:00 **The Judge and Bill** R | | 11:00 **Listen with Lidia** |
| 12 | 12:00 **Pets and Nutrition: Rabbits** | 12:00 **Movie: Rover's Friends** TVG ** A boy and his dog make new friends. | 12:00 **Adam Feather** R | 12:00 **Legal Cases** R | | 12:00 **The Mike Gracia Show** |
| 1 | | | | | | |
| 2 | | | | | | |

UNIT 10 • Lesson 19    99

# Lesson 19 AFTER READING

## Tuesday Evening

**READING COMPREHENSION**

**Sum It Up** is a reading strategy. Use it for a quick, overall understanding of what you read.

**READING COMPREHENSION**

A good way to understand what you read is to think through small reading pieces.

**CRITICAL THINKING**

**Trial and Error** is a thinking tool. To use Trial and Error, try something. If it doesn't work, try another idea. Keep doing these steps until you find something that works.

**Reading Comprehension**

**Read the TV Schedule on page 99. Then answer the questions below.**

1. **Sum It Up:** What type of shows are on each channel?

   Channel 15 _____    Channel 19 _____

   Channel 23 _____    Channel 25 _____

   Channel 29 _____    Channel 33 _____

2. **What You Think:** Circle the small print at the top of the TV schedule. Some of this information is in the chart below. Read each part. In your own words, write the meaning of each part.

| TV Schedule Key | What You Think This Means |
|---|---|
| Pay channels shaded | A |
| R—Rerun | B |
| Movie Key | C |
| TVG—All Viewers | D |
| TV14—Parental Attention Needed | E |
| TVMA—Mature audiences | F |
| Ratings from **** (excellent) to * (poor) | G |

3. **Trial and Error:** Work with a group of five classmates. On your own paper, write five shows your group wants to watch from 6:00 P.M. until 10:00 P.M.

100   UNIT 10 • Lesson 19

4. **Group Ideas:** You can guess at some types of TV shows by reading the show titles. Read the two types of shows below. Then find TV show names to match from page 99. Write the names where they belong below.

| Ball Games | How-To Shows |
|---|---|
| A _____ | D _____ |
| B _____ | E _____ |
| C _____ | F _____ |

What is a type of show that you like? _____

## Letters and Sounds Review

**Make a Word Find. To do this, follow the steps below.**

1. Read the Writing box on the left.
2. On a piece of paper, write ten words with silent letters. You can use words with silent letters from this book. You will use your ten words in your Word Find.
3. To make your Word Find, use a piece of graph paper. Write each word on the graph paper. Write one letter in a square. Your words can read across, down, or diagonally.
4. Add letters to all the empty squares. Draw a box around your Word Find.
5. Trade your Word Find with a classmate. Find and circle the hidden words.

## Language

**Read the sentences below. Then circle the correct word to make each sentence past tense.**

1. I (watch, watched) *Ben's Town* every week.
2. I (forgot, will forget) to record *Denver Friends*.
3. Chin Rohn (stars, starred) in *The Copy Man*.
4. *The World of Monkeys* (started, start) before *The National Dog Show* (ends, ended.)
5. Channel 16 (has, had) news on all day.
6. *Copper Pennies* (is, was) my sister's favorite show.
7. My uncle (get, got) that lamp from the *TV Shopping* channel.
8. When I was little, I (watched, watches) *Rick's Animals* every day.

---

### WRITING

A Word Find has lots of letters. At first, you may not see any words. Look closely to find words across, down, and diagonally. Circle any hidden words.

Here is an example of a Word Find.

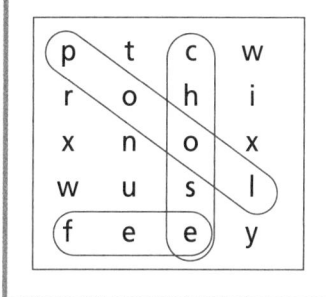

| p | t | c | w |
|---|---|---|---|
| r | o | h | i |
| x | n | o | x |
| w | u | s | l |
| f | e | e | y |

### LANGUAGE

A verb in **past tense** shows an action done in the past. Below are two sentences in past tense:

■ I opened the mail.
■ The little girl ate her meal

**LIFE SKILLS**

Watching TV shows can be fun. However, it is a good idea to enjoy a variety of activities.

**Life Skills Focus**

**What It Stands For:** Write ten fun activities you could do instead of watching TV. Circle your top three favorite activities.

1. _____
2. _____
3. _____
4. _____
5. _____
6. _____
7. _____
8. _____
9. _____
10. _____

# Lesson 20 BEFORE READING

## Your Own TV Schedule

**WORD SKILLS**

A singular noun tells about one person, place, or thing.

A plural noun tells about more than one person, place, or thing. Most plural nouns are made by adding **s** to a noun.

- **Singular nouns:** teacher, lake, boat
- **Plural nouns:** teachers, lakes, boats

### Word Skills

**Read the words below. Then write the plurals where they belong. One has been done for you.**

1. car, _cars_
2. road, _____
3. friend, _____
4. tree, _____
5. CD, _____
6. actor, _____

**Read the sentences below. Rewrite each sentence and use the possessive of the noun. One has been done for you.**

1. Kyle owns that car. _That is Kyle's car._
2. The squirrel lives in that tree. _____
3. Carly is the sister of Tim. _____

**WORD SKILLS**

A possessive noun shows ownership or a relationship.

A singular possessive noun ends in **'s**.

- **Ownership:**
  Rosa owns that ball.
  That is **Rosa's** ball.
- **Relationship:**
  Nick is the brother of Devon.
  Nick is **Devon's** brother.

### Use What You Know

**Find a TV schedule for one evening. Tape, staple, or glue the schedule to page 104. Then answer the questions below.**

1. Where did you get the TV schedule from?
   _____

2. How do you usually find out what is on TV channels?
   _____

3. Why do you think TV schedules are put out each week, and not every month?
   _____

UNIT 10 • Lesson 20   103

## Lesson 20 READING   Your Own TV Schedule

**Find a TV Schedule for one day. Tape, staple, or glue the schedule to this page.**

# Lesson 20 AFTER READING

## Your Own TV Schedule

**Reading Comprehension**

**Read the TV Schedule on page 104. Then answer the questions below.**

1. **Sum It Up:** Some TV channels show a certain type of show. Find four of these channels. Then write the channel numbers and the types of shows below.

   **A** Channel _____  _____

   **B** Channel _____  _____

   **C** Channel _____  _____

   **D** Channel _____  _____

2. **What You Think:** Write the number of one TV channel that you think is well liked. _____

   Why did you choose this TV channel?

   _____

   _____

   _____

3. **Trial and Error:** Work with a group of five classmates. On your own paper, choose TV shows to watch in the evening from 6:00 until 10:00. Work together on a schedule. Choose shows that you all find interesting and everyone wants to watch.

4. **Group Ideas:** Think of four groups to sort the shows into from Item 3 above. Write the name of each group below.

   **A** _____

   **B** _____

   **C** _____

   **D** _____

UNIT 10 • Lesson 20    105

**Language Review**

**Read the sentences below. Are they past or present tense? Circle the correct answer.**

1. Matt broke his hand playing ball.  past  present
2. School is done for the day.  past  present
3. I said I would not go.  past  present

**Write sentences about TV shows to match the verb tenses below. Be sure the subjects and verbs agree so that the sentences are correct.**

4. (present) _____

5. (past) _____

6. (past) _____

### WRITING

Understanding how to do a task helps you get the task done.

**Writing**

TV schedule writers must fit schedules in small spaces. In your own words, write five steps the TV schedule writers took to make the schedule on page 104. When you are done, proofread your work. Make any changes.

1. _____

2. _____

3. _____

4. _____

5. _____

106   UNIT 10 • Lesson 20

## CAREER

People who write about the movies for TV schedules use very few words. The writers try to tell a lot about the TV shows in a small space. People read these words to help them decide which TV shows to watch.

**Career Connection**

**Think of four movies you have seen. Write the title of each movie below. Then write about each movie, but keep your writing to 50 spaces or less. Each blank space or letter is one space.**

Movie Title _____

_____

— — — — — — — — — — — — — — — — — — — —

— — — — — — — — — — — — — — — — — — — —

— — — — — — — — — —


Movie Title _____

_____

— — — — — — — — — — — — — — — — — — — —

— — — — — — — — — — — — — — — — — — — —

— — — — — — — — — —


Movie Title _____

_____

— — — — — — — — — — — — — — — — — — — —

— — — — — — — — — — — — — — — — — — — —

— — — — — — — — — —


Movie Title _____

_____

— — — — — — — — — — — — — — — — — — — —

— — — — — — — — — — — — — — — — — — — —

— — — — — — — — — —

UNIT 10 • Lesson 20

# UNIT 11: ROAD MAPS

## Lesson 21 BEFORE READING

# Maps of Connecticut

### PHONICS

A word can have one or more syllables. A syllable has at least one vowel.

Many syllables and short words have the **CVCe** (consonant-vowel-consonant-silent e) pattern. The **vowel** is usually long and the **e** is usually silent.

### VOCABULARY

**compass rose**
drawing that shows the four main directions on a map

**legend**
list of symbols that stand for information on a map

**map**
drawing that shows the location of places in an area

**road map**
drawing that shows the highways, freeways, and roads between places

## Letters and Sounds

**Read the words in the box. Then write the words where they belong below. Some words go in both columns.**

| tin     | bedroom | plane  | won     | brave | sat   |
|---------|---------|--------|---------|-------|-------|
| mistake | contest | rope   | bonfire | like  | woke  |
| wisdom  | strike  | nut    | man     | alone | drive |

*CVC* in Whole Word or First Syllable

_____  _____

_____  _____

_____  _____

_____  _____

_____  _____

*CVCe* Pattern in Whole Word or Second Syllable

_____  _____

_____  _____

_____  _____

_____  _____

_____  _____

## Use What You Know

**Answer the questions below.**

1. Have you ever taken a road trip to another city?   Yes   No

2. If yes, did you use a road map to get there?   Yes   No

3. The top map of Connecticut on page 109 shows some of the cities in the state. How many cities do you think are on the map? _____

## Lesson 21 READING   Maps of Connecticut

### MASSACHUSETTS

Litchfield · Hartford · Tolland · Windham

**HARTFORD** ✱
Vernon
91   84

372

**WATERBURY** ·
New Haven
· Middletown
Middlesex
· Norwich
New London

Danbury ·
Fairfield
8   9   11   52   32   95

· **NEW HAVEN**
· New London

25

Fairfield ·
**BRIDGEPORT**
15

*Long Island Sound*

Greenwich · Stamford

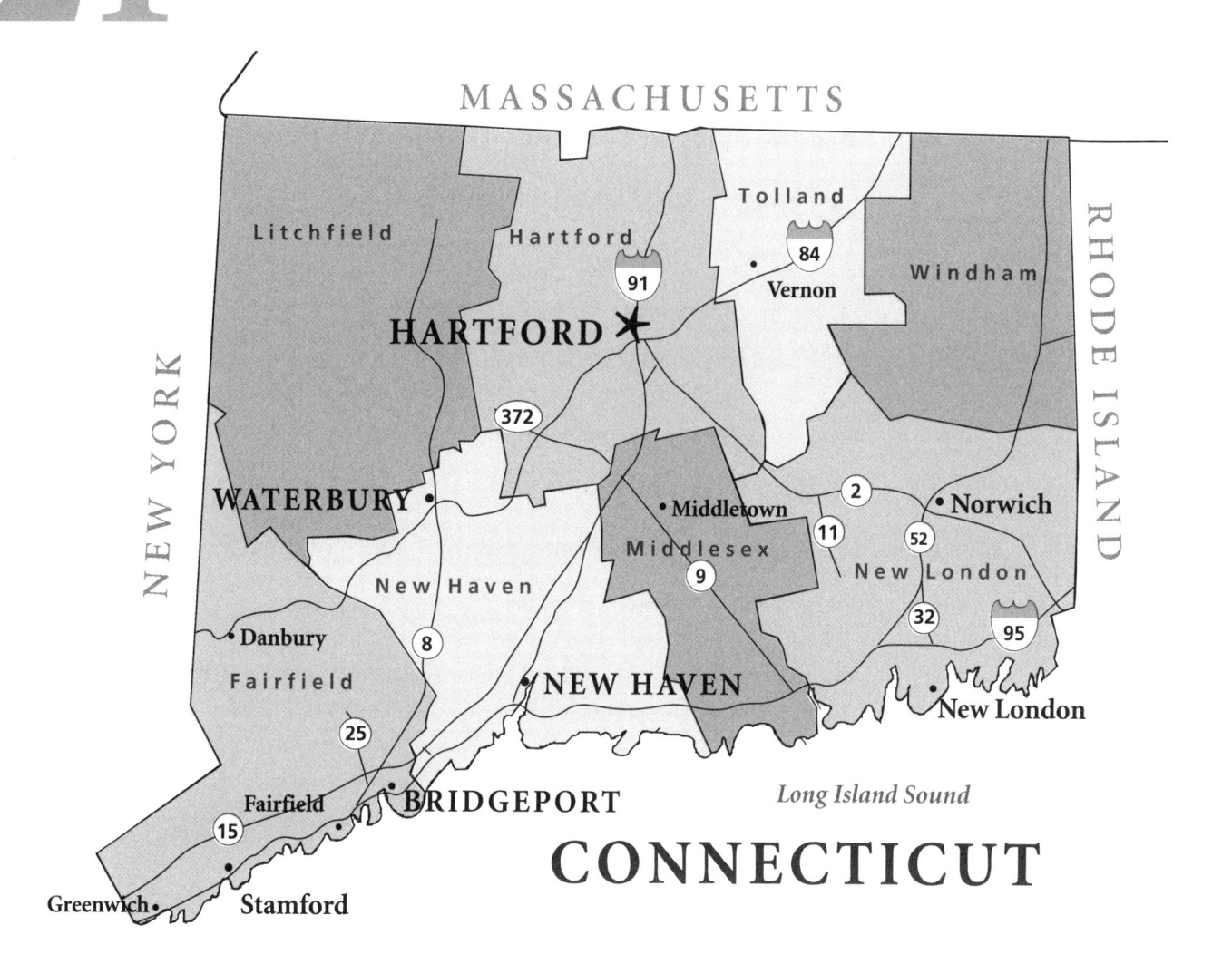

## CONNECTICUT

NEW YORK

RHODE ISLAND

**LEGEND**
- · City
- ✱ Capital
- ▬ Highway
- ■ Point of Interest

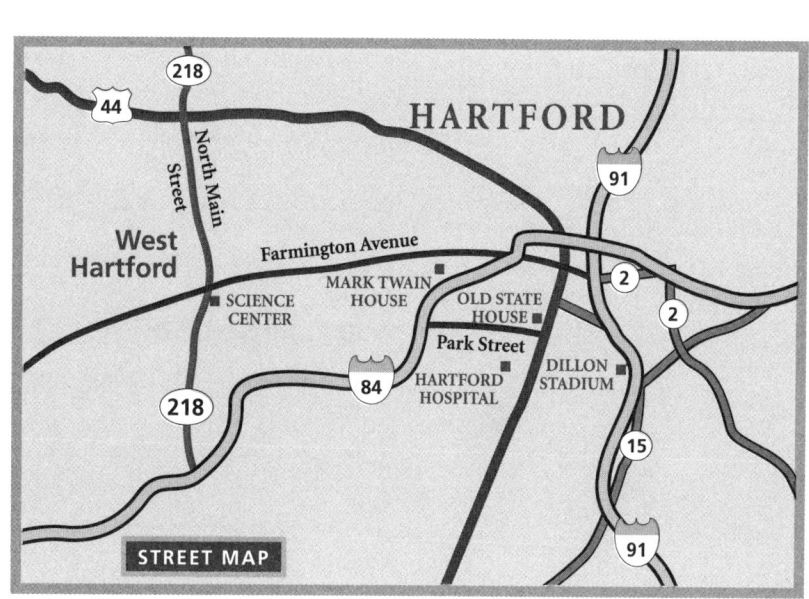

N / W / E / S

### HARTFORD

44   218
North Main Street
West Hartford
Farmington Avenue
91
SCIENCE CENTER
MARK TWAIN HOUSE
OLD STATE HOUSE
Park Street
2
84
HARTFORD HOSPITAL
DILLON STADIUM
218
15
91

**STREET MAP**

UNIT 11 • Lesson 21   109

# Lesson 21 AFTER READING: Maps of Connecticut

**READING COMPREHENSION**

You read for details when you use a map to get somewhere. Read the details correctly, or you will go to the wrong place!

**STRATEGY**

Figuring out something helps you be aware of what you read.

**CRITICAL THINKING**

As you read, write down key details. This helps you remember important facts. You can also organize the key facts for your use.

## Reading Comprehension

**Read the maps on page 109. Then answer the questions below.**

1. **Figure It Out:** The smaller map is a street map. When would you use a street map? _____

    The larger map is a road map. Why is a star in the middle of the road map? _____

2. **Read for Details:** Look at the street map.

    **A** Is Farmington Avenue north or south of Highway 84? _____

    **B** Is Dillon Stadium west or east of Hartford Hospital? _____

3. **Brainstorm:** Write three ways to find out about things to do in Hartford, Connecticut.

    **A** _____

    **B** _____

    **C** _____

4. **Organize Ideas:** Look at the road map.

    **A** Write directions to drive from Norwich to Danbury.

    _____
    _____
    _____

    **B** Look at the street map. Write directions to drive from the Science Center to Old State House.

    _____
    _____
    _____

110  UNIT 11 • Lesson 21

## Letters and Sounds Review

Why did Jules turn left at Water Street? Use the clues to solve the puzzle. Some words have the CVCe pattern in the last word or in the whole word.

### Clues
1. To get away
2. A long walk
3. 6th month
4. Past tense of write
5. To cook a cake
6. Protected
7. To turn completely around; like Earth
8. Yellow dairy food
9. To see a person and know him or her
10. Change a little
11. People want chocolate because they like the _____.
12. To thrill
13. One less than 100

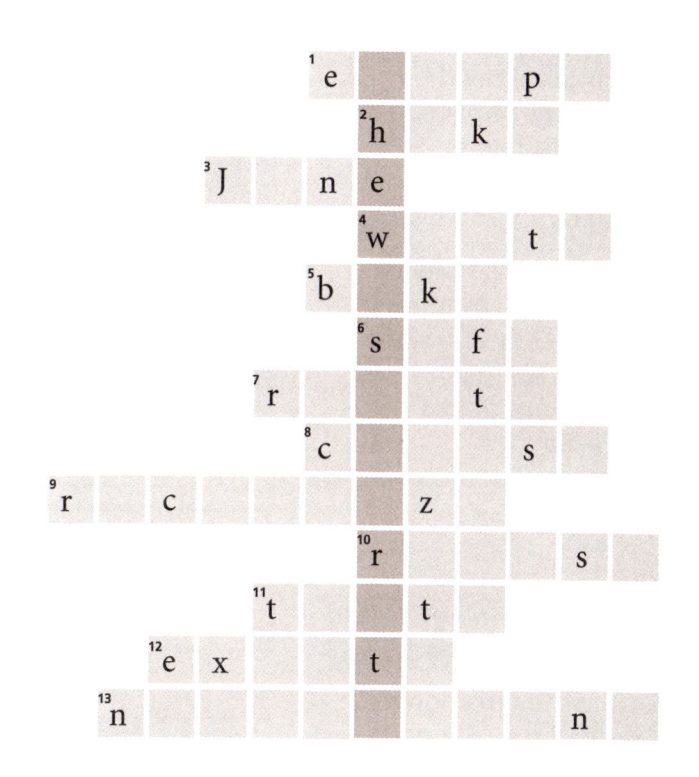

---

### LANGUAGE

A verb in **future tense** shows an action taking place in the future. Below are two sentences in future tense.

- I will talk to you after dinner.
- Olga will study with me tonight.

## Language

Read the sentences below. Then circle the words to make the sentences future tense.

1. We (go, will go, went) to Hartford next year.
2. Before we leave, we (study, studied, will study) the map.
3. We (write, wrote, will write) our plan on paper.
4. We (will put, put, puts) a map in the car.
5. The person in the front seat (reads, read, will read) the map.
6. The people in the back (will help, helped, help).
7. We (sleep, slept, will sleep) in our car.
8. We (eat, will eat, ate, ) in our car during the trip.
9. At night, we (will watch, watched, watch) movies.
10. Raja changed his mind. He (drive, will drive, drove,) the van.

UNIT 11 • Lesson 21

## LIFE SKILLS

Road maps show the roads and highways that connect communities. They also can show the locations of parks, airports, rivers, highway rest stops, and campgrounds.

Street maps show the streets and avenues in a city. They also show where to find important places in a city.

## LIFE SKILLS

To write directions for a road trip, put each new road on a new line. This makes the directions easier to follow.

### Life Skills Focus

**Write directions from where you live to the capital of your state. If needed, use a road map or a street map. Start a new line for each road.**

# Lesson 22 BEFORE READING: Your Own Road Map

## WORD SKILLS

Most plural nouns end in **s** or **es**. Some plural nouns follow other rules.

- Add **es** to words that end in **sh, ch, s, x,** or **z**.
  **Examples:** rashes, ranches, passes, faxes

- For words that end in consonant + **y**, change the **y** to **i**. Then add **es**.
  **Examples:** ladies, skies

- Some nouns that end in **f** or **fe** change the **f** to **v**. Then add **s** or **es**.
  **Examples:** leaves, knives

- Some words have unusual plurals.
  **Examples:** women, deer, mice, sheep

### Word Skills

**Read the words below. Then write the plurals where they belong.**

1. coach, _____
2. baby, _____
3. scarf, _____
4. child, _____
5. man, _____
6. foot, _____

**Read the sentences below. Then rewrite each sentence and use the possessive of the noun.**

1. That map belongs to Jose. _____

2. That chain holds the swing. _____

3. Van is the aunt of Mai. _____

### Use What You Know

**Make a copy of a road map of your area or state. Tape, staple, or glue the copy to page 114. Then answer the questions below.**

1. Have you or a family member used this road map?   Yes   No

2. What are two types of maps other than road maps?

   A _____

   B _____

# Lesson 22 READING   Your Own Road Map

**Make a copy of a road map of your area or state. Then tape, staple, or glue the copy to this page.**

# Lesson 22 AFTER READING

## Your Own Road Map

**STRATEGY**

**Study Pictures** is a reading strategy. It shows that pictures can be just as important as words.

### Reading Comprehension

**Read the map on page 114. Then answer the questions below.**

1. **Study Pictures:** Are there small pictures on the map?   Yes   No

   If yes, how many? _____

   Write what two of the small pictures mean.

   _____

   _____

   _____

   _____

**LIFE SKILLS**

A scale of miles is a drawing that shows how much distance an inch of space on a map stands for.

Below is scale of miles

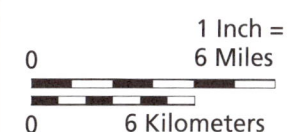

1 Inch =
0     6 Miles

0     6 Kilometers

2. **Read for Details:** What length on the map equals one mile? _____

   How many miles equal four inches on the map? _____

3. **Brainstorm:** Write five reasons why you might use this map.

   A _____

   B _____

   C _____

   D _____

   E _____

4. **Organize Ideas:** Choose a far north place on the map. Then choose a far south place. On your own paper, write driving directions from the southern to the northern place.

   Now choose a far west place on the map. Then choose a far east place. On your own paper, write driving directions from the eastern to the western place.

UNIT 11 • Lesson 22

## LANGUAGE

You may need help when you think about verb tenses. To help, try completing these sentences:

Yesterday, I _____

Today, I _____

Tomorrow, I _____

## Language Review

**Read the chart below. Then write the verbs in the correct tense below. One has been done for you.**

| Past Tense | Present Tense | Future Tense |
|---|---|---|
| cried | cry | will cry |
| 1. _____ | walk | 2. _____ |
| 3. _____ | 4. _____ | will sneeze |
| owned | 5. _____ | 6. _____ |
| 7. _____ | allows | 8. _____ |
| 9. _____ | 10. _____ | will drive |
| 11. _____ | throw | 12. _____ |

## Writing

Write two or more tips in your journal about learning to read better. For ideas, look in this book from pages 58 to 117. Look at the boxes on the pages. Choose two or more helpful tips.

In your own words, write why they are helpful to you. When you are done, read what you have written. Be sure it says what you mean.

## CAREER

Map companies make new road maps. New road maps are needed because information changes. Some changes are because of:

- New roads
- Road upgrades
- Road name changes
- Other name changes, such as a park
- New major developments, such as a new hospital
- New areas for houses

Career Connection

**Work with two or three classmates. Role play that you own a map company. Look at your maps on page 114. Think of changes to make on a future map of your area or state. Write five changes below.**

1. _____

2. _____

3. _____

4. _____

5. _____

UNIT 11 • Lesson 22

# Lesson 23 BEFORE READING

## UNIT 12: PRODUCT INSTRUCTIONS

## Electronic Calculator

### VOCABULARY

**calculation**
the result of a mathematical operation

**decimal point**
the period that divides the whole part of a number from the fractional part

**electronic calculator**
a machine powered by electricity that can carry out mathematical functions

**entry**
numbers and operations entered into a calculator

**memory**
the ability to store information

**percentage**
part of a hundred

### Letters and Sounds

**Read each pair of CVCe words below. In each pair, circle the word with the long vowel sound.**

1. treasure
   beehive

2. notice
   plate

3. above
   blade

4. unite
   chance

5. give
   hive

6. divide
   chocolate

7. cage
   necklace

8. awake
   above

9. have
   beside

10. outside
    glove

11. shade
    done

12. come
    refuse

### Use What You Know

**Answer the questions below.**

1. When have you used an electronic calculator? _____

2. Think about when you have used a calculator. When you pressed a calculator key, did something unusual happen?   Yes   No

3. If yes, write about what happened. _____

118  UNIT 12 • Lesson 23

# Lesson 23 READING   Electronic Calculator

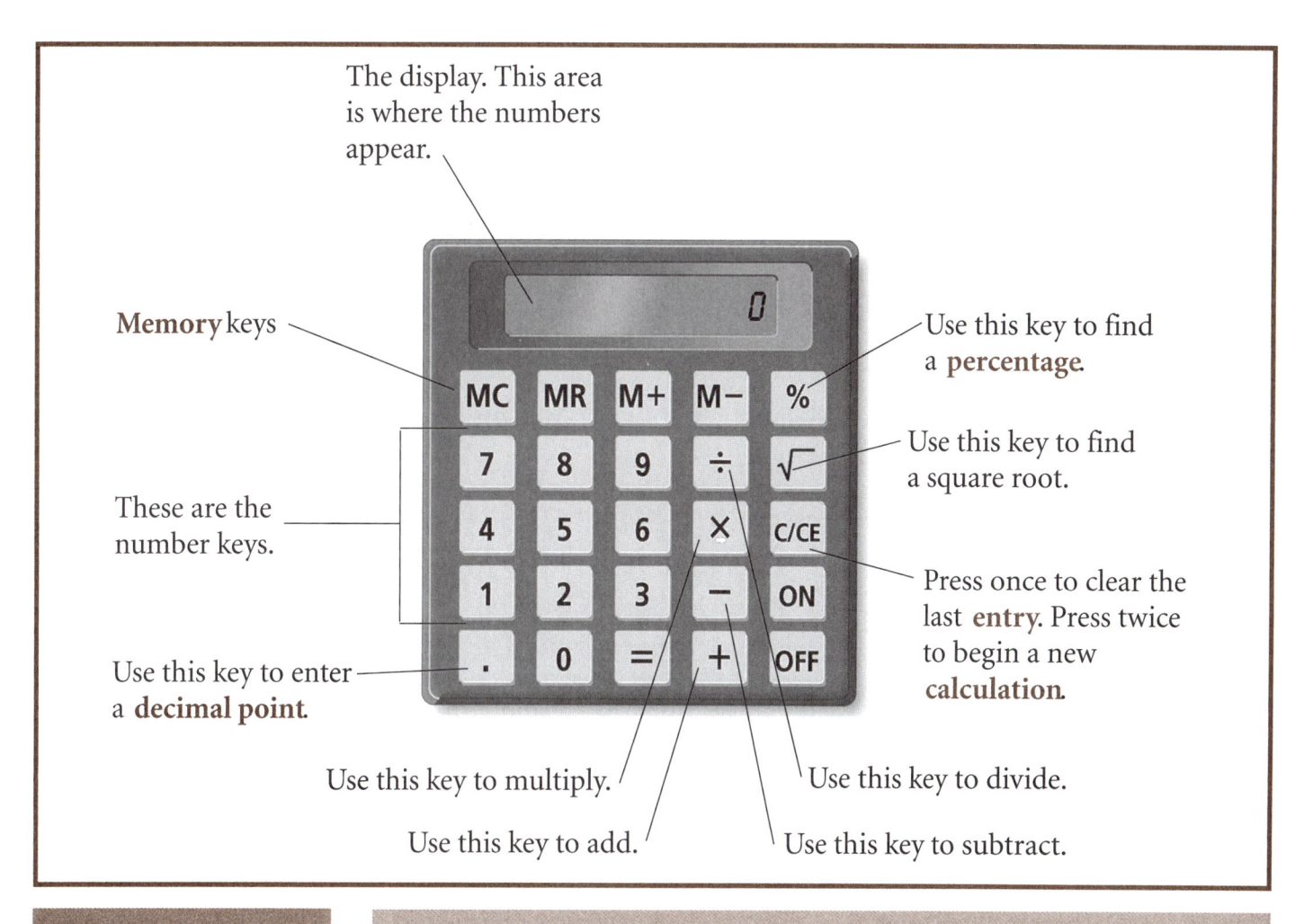

The display. This area is where the numbers appear.

**Memory** keys

These are the number keys.

Use this key to enter a **decimal point**.

Use this key to multiply.

Use this key to add.

Use this key to find a **percentage**.

Use this key to find a square root.

Press once to clear the last **entry**. Press twice to begin a new **calculation**.

Use this key to divide.

Use this key to subtract.

## LIFE SKILLS

The calculator above has the basic functions you find on most calculators. It also looks like many calculators.

You can use a calculator to help you do arithmetic. In many cases, you key the calculation the same way you would write it on paper.

You can use a calculator to help you do arithmetic quickly and accurately. In many cases, you key the calculation the same way you would write it on paper.

Press 23 + 61 =
The display will read 84.
23 + 61 = 84
Press 12 × 12 =
The display will read 144.
12 × 12 = 144

Press 98 − 18 =
The display will read 80.
98 − 18 = 80
Press 63 ÷ 9 =
The display will read 7.
63 ÷ 9 = 7

It is a good idea to look at the display after you key in each number. It helps to check that you have not pressed a wrong key by mistake.

## Lesson 23 AFTER READING

# Electronic Calculator

**STRATEGY**

Try putting context clues into a chart. This can help make what you read more clear.

## Reading Comprehension

**Read the information on page 119. Then answer the questions below.**

1. **Main Ideas and Details:** Look for details about the main idea below. One detail has been done for you. Write two more details.

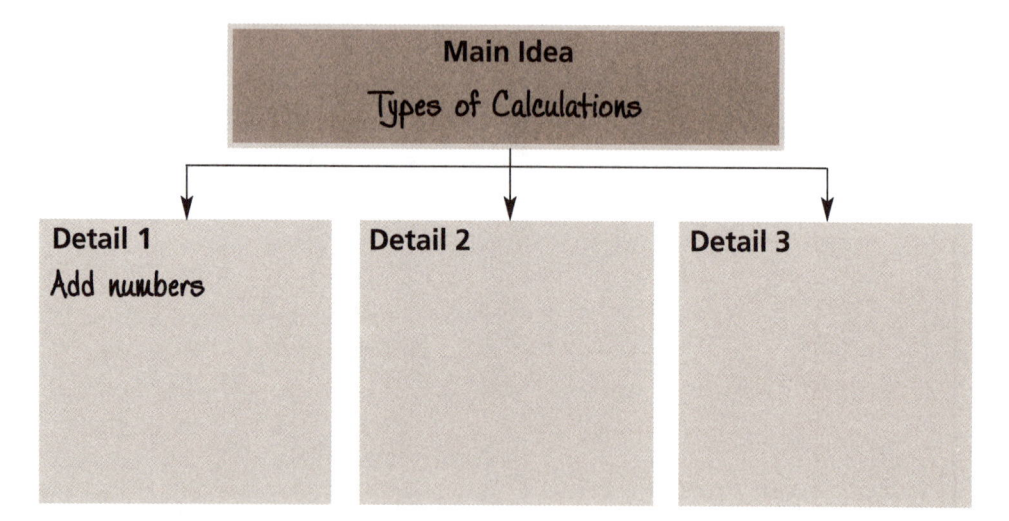

   **Main Idea**
   **Types of Calculations**

   | Detail 1 | Detail 2 | Detail 3 |
   |---|---|---|
   | Add numbers | | |

2. **Make Connections:** Write about three times when you would use an electronic calculator.

   **A** _____

   **B** _____

   **C** _____

3. **Cause and Effect:** Fill in the blanks below.

   **A** If you push the C/CE button once, then _____
   
   _____

   **B** If you push the _____ key, then the next number is added.

120 UNIT 12 • Lesson 23

**Letters and Sounds Review**

**Read the clues. Then write each CVCe word in the puzzle.**

Across
1. Gather leaves
4. Exchange or barter
6. Has four burners
8. What a clock tells
10. Clothes used in a play

Down
2. Not on time
3. To thrill
5. To be bold, not be afraid
7. Be part of an election
9. More than one mouse

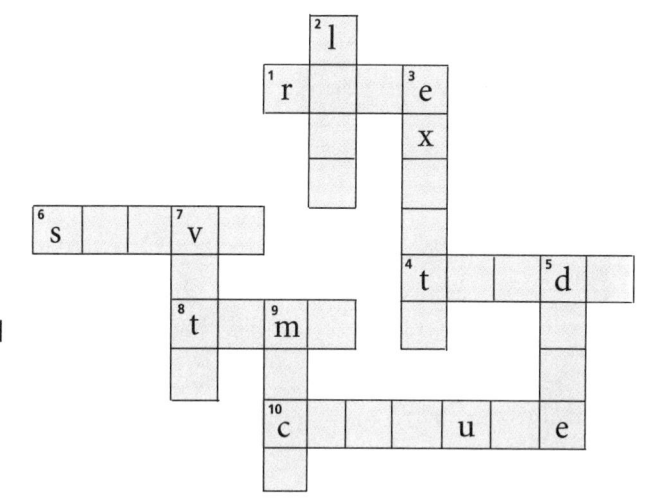

Language

**Write sentences using the nouns, verbs, and tenses below. One has been done for you.**

Jenna, eat, past tense: _Jenna ate two cookies._

1. rabbit, run, present tense: _____

2. pencil, fall, future tense: _____

3. Chao, swim, past tense: _____

4. Chris, skip, present tense: _____

5. eagle, fly, past tense: _____

6. Flute, play, future tense: _____

**LIFE SKILLS**

Keep a small calculator with your checkbook. It is also a good idea to bring one when you shop.

**LIFE SKILLS**

There are many kinds of electronic calculators. Each calculator is a little different from others. Some have more keys that others. The keys may be in different places. You may have to press the keys in a certain order. Most calculators, however, are very similar.

**Life Skills Focus**

**Alike and Different:** Think about the electronic calculator on page 119. Then think about the calculator that you use. It can be a hand calculator on a computer. How are they alike? How are they different? Write your answers in the chart below. If you do not know an answer, leave it blank.

| Questions | Electronic Calculator on page 119 | Calculator you use |
|---|---|---|
| 1. How long is the calculator? | A | B |
| 2. How wide is the calculator? | A | B |
| 3. Can the calculator print? | A | B |
| 4. Are the keys as big as your fingertips? | A | B |
| 5. How many keys are on the calculator? | A | B |
| 6. Does the calculator need batteries or solar power? | A | B |

# Lesson 24 BEFORE READING

## Your Own Product Instructions

### WORD SKILLS

More than one person, place, or thing can own something.

- If the plural ends in **s**, add an **'** after the **s**.
  **Example:** trees' leaves

- If the plural ends in another letter, add **'s**.
  **Example:** men's shirts

### Word Skills

**Fill in the blanks in the chart.**

| Singular Noun | Singular Possessive Noun | Plural Noun | Plural Possessive Noun |
|---|---|---|---|
| goose | goose's | geese | geese's |
| 1. | person's | 2. | 3. |
| 4. | 5. | teeth | 6. |
| boy | 7. | 8. | 9. |
| 10. | 11. | deer | 12. |
| 13. | 14. | 15. | chair's |

### Use What You Know

Find instructions for a household appliance. Make a copy of one page of the instructions. Tape, staple, or glue the copy to page 124. Then answer the questions below.

1. What type of product goes with these instructions? _____

2. Do you know how to use this product without instructions?  Yes  No

3. How many of your classmates have used this type of a product before? _____

UNIT 12 • Lesson 24

## Lesson 24 READING Your Own Product Instructions

**Find instructions for a household appliance. Make a copy of one page of the instructions. Tape, staple, or glue the copy to this page.**

# Lesson 24 AFTER READING: Your Own Product Instructions

## Reading Comprehension

**Read the instructions on page 124. Then answer the items below.**

1. **Use Context Clues:** Write three words from page 124 that are hard for you to read. Write words in the sentence or before or after the sentence that give clues to the word meaning. Leave boxes blank if there are no clues. Then write the meanings of the words.

| Hard to Read Word | Some Words in Sentence | Words in Sentence Before or After | What You Think This Word Means |
|---|---|---|---|
| A | | | |
| B | | | |
| C | | | |

2. **Main Ideas and Details:** Choose a main idea from page 124. Write it in the top box. Add three details in the other boxes. If you need help, see page 120.

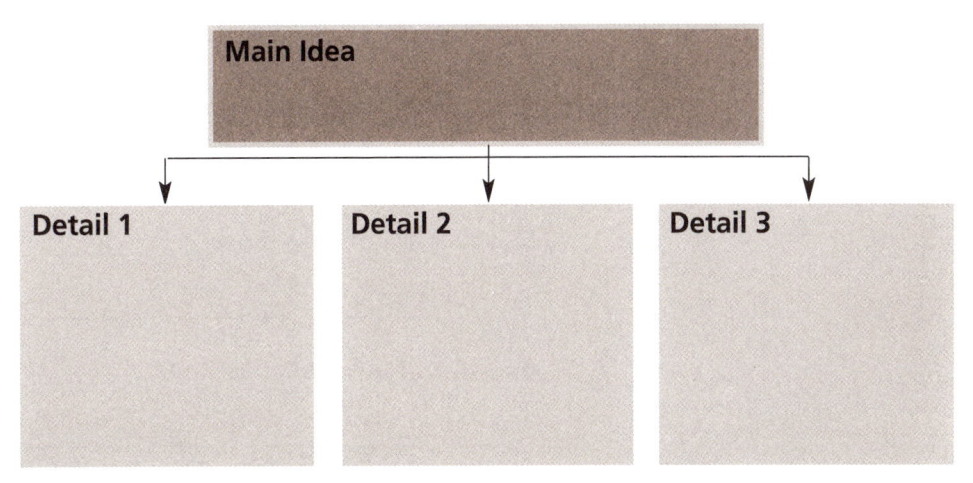

**Main Idea**

Detail 1    Detail 2    Detail 3

3. **Make Connections:** Write three reasons you might use the product that goes with the instructions on page 124.

A _____

B _____

C _____

**4. Alike and Different:** Complete the empty boxes.

| One way the instructions on pages 119 and 124 are **alike** is | ➡ | |
|---|---|---|

| | ➡ | |
|---|---|---|

## Language Review and Writing

**Write sentences that use the nouns, verbs, and tenses below. Use active voice in all your sentences. When you are done, proofread your work. Make any changes. One has been done for you.**

team members, run, past tense: *The team members ran a good race.*

1. Lisa, smile, present tense: _____

2. I, know, future tense: _____

3. Bill and Teresa, remember, past tense: _____

4. cats, play, present tense: _____

5. you, find, future tense: _____

6. computer, break, past tense: _____

7. Dominic, forget, present tense: _____

8. cars, follow, future tense: _____

**CAREER**

People who work with numbers a lot often use an electronic calculator. They can use a calculator without looking at the keys. This is called knowing how to 10-key.

## Career Connection

**Look in the help wanted or job section of your local newspaper or on the Internet. Find four ads to hire people who can 10-key. Cut out or make a copy of the job ads. Then tape, staple, or glue the job ads to this page.**

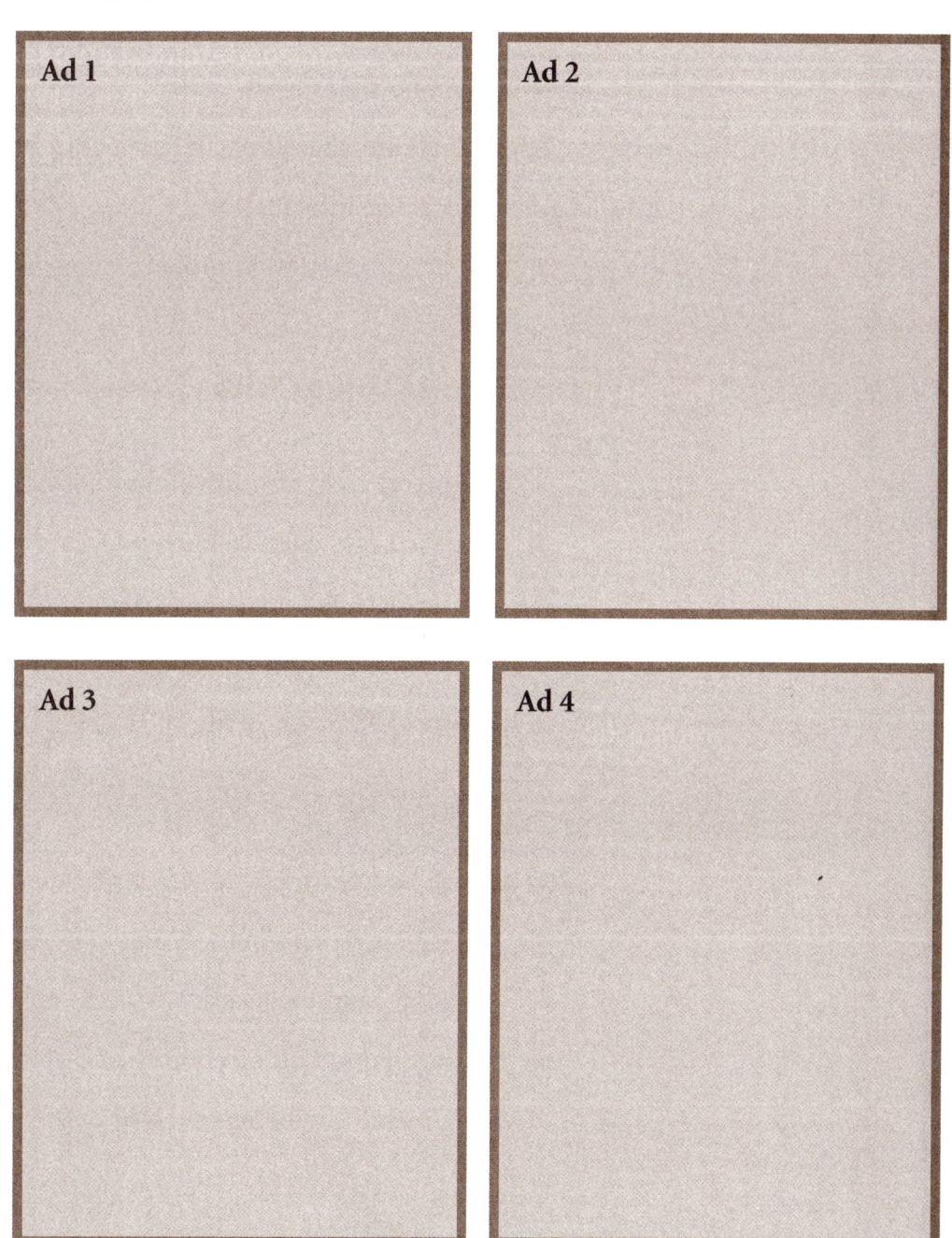

**Ad 1**

**Ad 2**

**Ad 3**

**Ad 4**

UNIT 12 • Lesson 24

## SUMMARY OF SKILLS AND STRATEGIES

Look back at what you've learned in this book.

### Reading Skills
You learned to…

- read words with letters that work together in different ways
- look at how words are built
- think about what you will read before you start to read
- sort and use information
- look at information in more than one way

### Language and Writing Skills
You learned to…

- use correct capitalization and punctuation
- write facts and creative ideas
- sum up facts and ideas, and to use active voice
- use space wisely and write in a journal
- proofread what you write

### Life and Career Skills
You learned how reading and writing relates to….

- planning personal finances and daily household chores
- being safe, making healthy choices, and traveling
- making plans, making choices, and getting along with people
- enjoying life and being involved in the world around you